Skin Spirits: Animal Parts in Spiritual and Magical Practice

By Lupa

Praise for Lupa's Books

[*DIY Totemism*] is a clear, concise guide to working with animal totems which answers both the simple and difficult questions about totemism… If you are interested in working with animal totems, this book will be an excellent starting place: if you already have some experience, you will find many useful techniques and theories… -Kenaz Filan, author of *The Haitian Vodou Handbook* and reviewer for *newWitch* magazine

Certainly her approach is anything goes, try it and see…[*DIY Totemism*] is a new way of approaching the subject and as such I would recommend it to anyone interested in exploring the topic from a practical perspective. –Nina Lazarus, reviewer for the Esoteric Book Review, http://esotericbookreview.wordpress.com

Lupa [the editor] has made an effort to assemble a wide variety of viewpoints in [*Talking About the Elephant*]… Among the reasons I like books from this company are the wide diversity of topics and the fact that, agree with the authors or not, I always find my ideas being challenged. --Mike Gleason, prolific independent reviewer

[*Fang and Fur, Blood and Bone* is] a practitioner's book, and it comes as a welcome relief from other books in the occult field…groundbreaking, intelligent, and gives its reader concepts that work. –Diana Rajchel, reviewer for Facing North, http://www.facingnorth.net

[*Fang and Fur, Blood and Bone*] is an excellent book for people wishing to delve into the worlds of animal magics. It is far better than any other book I have read on the subject, avoiding the rote use of listing animal correspondences and getting down to the nitty-gritty of actual rituals and meditations fully accessible to even a novice. –W. Lyon Martin, Magickware.wordpress.com

Skin Spirits: Animal Parts in Spiritual and Magical Practice

By Lupa

Megalithica Books

Stafford, England

Cover Art: Lupa
Cover Design: Andy Bigwood
Interior Photos and Artwork in Photos: Lupa
Editor: Taylor Ellwood
Copy editor: Kiya Nicoll
Layout: Lupa
Foreword: Edward Dain

Set in Book Antiqua and Nyala

Megalithica Books Edition 2009

A Megalithica Books Publication
http://www.immanion-press.com
info@immanion-press.com
8 Rowley Grove
Stafford ST17 9BJ
UK

ISBN 078-1-905713-34-9

Acknowledgements

As always, huge thanks to Taylor, Storm, Andy, and everyone else at Immanion/Megalithica for helping make this book a reality; you're a great group of folks to work with, especially when I'm being persnickety about things. Edward, your foreword is quite appreciated, and I'm glad to have it as the opener to this book; thank you for sharing your own experiences with this sort of spiritual and magical work. Kiya, you caught all kinds of little details in the copy edit that I much appreciate. Also, a shout-out to everyone at the FurHideandBone Livejournal community for the education, the lively conversation, and the shared appreciation. And finally, I want to acknowledge all my readers past, present and future, for making it worth my time to get all these thoughts converted to pixels.

Dedications

To Tay, for your love and patience over the past few years as we've navigated some rough times as well as enjoyed the best. Thank you for being at Ground Zero with me on a daily basis.

To S., for also being loving and patient through everything thus far, as well as being extra appreciative of my snarkasm. Also, swords. Mmmmm...swords...

Other Works by Lupa

Fang and Fur, Blood and Bone: A Primal Guide to Animal Magic (2006)

A Field Guide to Otherkin (2007)

Kink Magic: Sex Magic Beyond Vanilla (with Taylor Ellwood, 2007)

DIY Totemism: Your Personal Guide to Animal Totems (2008)

Talking About the Elephant: An Anthology of Neopagan Perspectives on Cultural Appropriation (editor, 2008)

Table of Contents

Foreword
By Edward Dain

You don't know me.

Or if you do, it almost certainly isn't by this name. I live in a closet full of brooms and leather that's big enough to fit a couple of partners in.

Then again, you might know me by this name, and even then you might be wondering why I, of all people, am writing this forward. Lupa originally asked me to contribute to *Kink Magic*, but the vagaries of life prevented from doing so. I have always regretted this, so I leapt at the chance to write a forward for a book on a subject that is near to my heart and my practice.

You likely haven't seen the two necklaces I wear everyday, or the third that gets dragged out for special occasions to shake and rattle its way through ritual. The number of people who've seen my current altar can be counted on one hand at this point in time.

You haven't seen the necklace of Tiger-eye and Bloodstone, the one that eats Kevlar and Tiger-tail at whim, and eventually chews through the multi-stranded flexwire with contemptuous ease. That necklace is meaningless for this discussion, so we'll leave it a nothing more than a passing mention.

But the necklace that people rear back from, the one that makes the barber, the chiropractor, the massage therapist, draw their hands back the first few times they see it and say, "What is that?" That is a necklace to talk about here.

A string of sixty-seven interlocking vertebrae that I wear around my neck, created from the bones of a serpent.

I have no idea what kind of snake it is, if it was venomous, if it was safe. The bones don't tell me that, and the serpent doesn't care anymore. It has shed its skin for the final time, shuffled off the mortal coil, and such petty concerns are beneath it now.

The bones are a deep golden yellow, burnished by years next to my skin, impregnated by my sweat, my tears, even my blood. They fit together, surface pitted with black, the edges polished ivory in places. The colors weave together like the triple golds of my wedding ring.

I could go on for paragraphs about the symbolism inherent in a necklace made from the bones of a serpent.

But that would be telling.

You figure it out. Breathe deep and raise the Kundalini, go down among the dead where Níðhögg gnaws, blink the venom from your eyes if you can and then walk with Wadjet out through the labyrinth...

You'll find yourself back again at the beginning like the Ouroboros.

Easy enough.

I can dangle the cord on the tip of finger and rattle them, those sixty-seven little bones and let the sound drop me into trance, let me sink into Mother's embrace and fly outside my body...

I dream of that wet, thick, snapping, crack that comes with a broken bone. Dream the heat of the cooking fire, the marrow being sucked out, and the scent of roast flesh. There are screams of birth and death, the sensation of standing in the dark of night clothed in nothing but the sky, the trickle of rich, warm blood as it drips down my body in bright and sanguinary display, and the slowing beat of my heart as the sound of wings fills my ears.

It is a good dream.

At night I can reach up above my head to the corner of bed and let my fingers play across the small bone skulls of the mala that hangs there. The small stylized skulls with crooked teeth and large sightless eyes are carved from something, cow or yak most likely, it's not traditional.

11

That would be human bone.

My fingers caress the beads of the mala, there are 100 small skulls on the main string and one more at the knot. Not a standard number, but it works well enough, and I have no need for the symbolism of 12 Houses and 9 Planets in my own work. As a third necklace it more often serves as a thick band of white bone around one wrist to pair with the thin band of stainless steel chain around the other.

Bone comes in many forms, some carved and some natural.

A skull sits on my altar. At times it sits on my bedside table, other times it sits quietly contained in the darkness and silk. For years it sat on my grandfather's worktable in his basement and when he died I claimed it. Moving it requires care, the jaw is still loose, and the yellowed texture of the bone is both smooth and rough to the touch at the same time.

But through the night it whispers in my ear of life, death, and the flawed understanding we all to often have of both states. It stares at me with sightless eyes, its gaze looking past the flesh and sinew to the bones beneath my skin, the skull that is a mirror-image of itself, and drinks in the passions it finds there, the viscera of my soul, the quintessence of my desire.

There's a certain liminal quality to shadows, almost by definition. It doesn't matter if they are inside or outside of us. The skulls remind me of impermanence. They give me a window to look inside, a track to follow as I look for a bit of the Mystery here or there along the way. A place to align eros and thanatos into peosis and praxis – to find in the intersection of the matching arcs of contemplation and action, the balance point of a lifetime spent in service to the Divine.

Lupa is giving you the opportunity to participate in a Work that is more primal with this text. That is not to say that it is better, just different and perhaps even more dangerous if you are foolish or careless. There is a deep end to this pool, and a shallow end, and ultimately you will only go where you choose to. It can be hard to dance with the spirits in this way in a manner that is respectful, and this is one of the situations where the spirits can be their most unforgiving.

They can also be their most rewarding.

Walk with respect.

D.

Introduction

Of all animals, humans are the most adept at using tools. Until relatively recently in our history as a species, all our tools were derived from either plant or animal sources. This includes both spiritual tools and practical, everyday objects. Whether we needed to cover our increasingly hairless bodies, kill ever-more-dangerous prey, or create better shelters, as we developed as a species, we innovated newer ways to get things done.

It could, of course, be argued that the first animal parts we made use of were edibles—meat, bone marrow, organs, and anything else we could use to nourish our bodies. However, we're hardly unique in this respect, and so I'd like to focus on using animal parts in a more permanent manner. Unfortunately, I've not been able to find any sort of comprehensive text or other collection of information on the historical, practical, and ceremonial uses of animal parts from cultures around the world, only brief mentions in bits and pieces of books on broader topics. Since I wanted to cover a lot more practical information in this text, what I've included on the historical information should not in any way be seen as exhaustive.

This practical information includes not only magical theories on working with the spirits in the remains, but also some hands-on projects for creating ritual tools and other sacred objects. If you choose to work through some of these projects, please take the opportunity to utilize the magical concepts I discuss in earlier chapters. Additionally, much of the specifically spiritual material may be used by those who may not feel artistically inclined. For the most part, I don't elaborate on the uses of the various ritual tools discussed; this is not a paganism 101 book, nor is it an in-depth exploration of a particular ritual style or pagan religion. Since I want to focus on the animal parts in specific, I assume that either A) you already have a basic understanding of tools commonly found in neopaganism, or B) you have access to that information through books, other people, the internet, etc. I try hard not to rehash material that's already been explained quite thoroughly elsewhere.

Please keep in mind that this book is primarily based on my own experiences. It is not meant to be taken as holy writ, and it is colored by my subjective perceptions. Therefore, if you encounter something different from what I describe here, you aren't necessarily wrong. In fact, I encourage people to explore beyond what I discuss in any of my books. A lot of what I write about tends to be topics that don't have a lot of existing practical material on them, and I would prefer that people use my writing as a jumping-off point for their own experimentation. If what I say works for you, great. If not, then happy exploring!

Animal remains are controversial, whether we're talking fur coats on the fashion runway, or pagans running around festivals with fox tails hanging off their belts. While I have my own perspectives on how to work with them, I would like to make it clear that every person has hir own ethical boundaries. You do not have to utilize every practice or project in this book in order to get something out of it. None of my books (to date, anyway) are step-by-step procedures where every chapter must be followed to the letter in order to complete a certain end result. Rather, what I offer are ideas that you are free to either integrate into your practice or not.

Speaking of controversy, I would like to note that although some of the projects in this book may be commonly mistaken as "Native American", I am not a member of any tribe, nor do I have any tribal ancestry. Because so many people in the Western world, particularly in the United States, associate various arts and crafts made from animal parts with American indigenous peoples, they often assume that these creations are automatically connected to those cultures. Additionally, some of the names for some of these items either come out of Native American languages (not always translated well), or are derived from quasi-Native-American pop culture and New Age spirituality.

Most cultures throughout history have utilized animal remains beyond food; however, because many of these cultures are no longer extant or shifted into industrial and post-industrial economies, the main examples we have of animal-based creations is from Native American cultures. And since most animal remains don't last more than a couple hundred years at best, we don't have very many examples of things made from them from cultures that abandoned their hunter-gatherer and/or agrarian tendencies centuries ago.

This means that no matter your genetic makeup, somewhere in your history you have people who made things out of skins, bones, and the like. So while individual styles may vary from culture to culture, working with animal parts is far from a "Native American thing". Of course, you're welcome to utilize elements of whatever culture(s) you are a part of. However, this book is offered from an American neopagan perspective, and the patterns in here are largely generic (such as drawstring bags). I've tried to avoid things that are specific to a particular culture, such as dreamcatchers.[1]

On a more administrative note, as much as I might have liked to have included color photos in this text, due to the type of printing Immanion/Megalithica uses, these would not have been cost-effective. Therefore I have endeavored to supply the best quality black and white photos that I could.

Finally, while a significant portion of this book contains how-to instructions for creating various ritual items, don't feel that you can't get anything out of this book if you just don't have

---

[1] In the United States it is illegal to misrepresent artistry not created by members of Native American tribes as being genuine "Native American artwork". Information on the Indian Arts and Crafts Act of 1990 may be found at http://www.artnatam.com/regist.html.

much in the way of artistic talent, or otherwise lack the resources for making these items. The rest of the material works just as well for things that were made by someone else. And hey—if you want, you're more than welcome to see what I've made for sale at http://www.thegreenwolf.com/artwork.html. (Never let it be said that I am above a little self-promotion.)

Lupa
Portland, OR
15 August, 2009

Chapter One: Why Work
With Animal Parts?

I've always been fascinated by animals—and not just the living ones. Early on, I found myself unafraid of their remains. I remember being a toddler and playing with a dried, flat toad that had been run over by a car. Later on, I amassed a small collection of rabbit skulls and feathers that "mysteriously" disappeared when my family moved to a new home. I envied a friend of mine whose father had bought her a pine marten skin from a souvenir shop, and I looked longingly at taxidermy mounts at homes and businesses over the years. It's not that I wanted to kill animals; it was simply that, being raised in a small town but not in the most rural areas, my exposure to animals was quite limited. No one ever took me hunting or camping, and when I fished I only did catch and release. My knowledge about the natural world primarily came from the small patches of woods and a lot of books. To me, having the remains of the animals gave me a connection to something I could never really touch otherwise.

It wasn't until I was in college in the late 1990s that I was able to really satiate my curiosity about skins and bones, and start a collection for keeps. I had learned how to make loomed beadwork in an applied arts class in high school, and one year, as I was doing my university work, I yearned to bead again. I dug out my supplies, though I found I was limited to only three colors of beads. At the suggestion of an acquaintance I drove over to the next small town and found a shop there that catered to the local powwow circuit. Not only did they have more beads than I could ever imagine, but they had skins, turtle shells, claws and other animal parts. And I had a job and a checking account.

I think you can guess what happened next.

At first I just wanted some leather to stitch my beads to, making decorated pouches and chokers. However, I soon branched out. In the years following this creative outlet, I collected a pretty sizable variety of remains. When I moved to Pittsburgh, PA in 2001, I found myself within driving distance of two large flea markets where I found skins, fur coats, taxidermy mounts, and other things. Additionally, the local thrift stores were generally good for fur coats and stoles. I continued to make pouches and jewelry, and also started creating ritual tools, wall hangings, and even ceremonial headdresses and other costumery.

For the first few years, this was primarily an artistic endeavor. However, over time I began to notice the energy of the parts more often. So I started paying closer attention as I worked with them. I noticed soon after that what I perceived wasn't just energy, but spirits. I began to talk to them about what they wanted their remains to become. They generally weren't too happy about being trophies and expensive coats — no one really appreciated them for what they actually were. I made it a point to give them better afterlives than that, and started saying prayers over each completed piece that it would go to someone who would love it and cherish it for who and what it was.

In 2004 I was driving with a friend of mine to a pagan festival. We were talking about magic (as we so often did) and somehow we got onto the subject of skin spirits. I began to explain to him what it was that I did, and why. He found it exceptionally interesting, and he encouraged me to write a book about it. Enthused, I managed to write out an outline — and then promptly got distracted by numerous disastrous events that occurred that summer.

However, only a few months later, distressed by my job and wanting to do something more with myself, I pulled out the outline and in the space of about three weeks typed out the rough draft of what would become my first book, *Fang and Fur, Blood and Bone: A Primal Guide to Animal Magic*. It featured an entire chapter on my work with skin spirits, which would become one of the most popular chapters.

I began writing this book over two years after *Fang and Fur* came out in 2006. In Autumn of 2007, I finally listened to the spirits that had been poking and prodding me towards a more formal shamanic path for several years. Part of my practice (which I tagged with the name therioshamanism, "animal shamanism"), involved deeper work with animal parts, especially a collection of skins that I sometimes danced with over the years. However, the spirits also approved of the idea of passing on more detailed methods of working with skin spirits in specific. While I don't want to encourage people to go out and kill animals just for their skins and bones, I do want to promote a better way of treating the remains of those that are killed. I'll detail more of that in chapter three.

Traditional Uses of Animal Parts[2]

Humans have been utilizing animal parts for almost as long as we've been using tools. From the first clothing, to materials for hunting and household goods, bones, skins, and other animal parts have been integrated into human lifestyles for millennia. Today the uses may be less visible—fur coats are less common than, say, gelatin made with hooves and hides, or estrogen-replacement drugs made from the urine of pregnant mares.[3] On

---

[2] This is a very brief and by no means complete treatment of the history of human use of non-human animal remains outside of food. I toyed with the idea of trying to do a much more thorough and complete exploration, but that would take a book in and of itself! (Not that I haven't rejected the idea of trying it some day…) However, since this is primarily a practical text, please forgive the brief and relatively narrow set of examples.

[3] Incidentally, if you're unfamiliar with the processes by which the urine is collected, you may be surprised at some of the alleged cruelty involved. More information may be found at http://www.hsus.org/horses_equines/issues/the_facts_about_premarin.html

the other hand, in addition to eating a lot of meat, modern Americans, at least, seem to be quite fond of leather coats, shoes, bags, and other items. However, our fondness is more a luxury than a necessity, and reflects mass-production as opposed to hand-crafted creations.

Unfortunately, because animal parts decay relatively easily, it's hard to get decent information on older pagan cultures' use of animal remains. Indigenous cultures, particularly those of North America, seem to be the best modern examples of traditional uses of animal parts. I've discussed a number of these in the chapters on hides and bones. It shouldn't be assumed, of course, that indigenous people all walk around in deerskin clothing and feathered headdresses, but there are members of those cultures who continue traditional crafting of such things for ceremonial and personal use.

Hides

The preserved (tanned, salted, etc.) skins of animals, most often mammals, have played a key role in the development of humanity as a species. For many groups of humans, these composed the first clothing we had as we evolved less hair on our bodies. While no doubt the first attempts at preserving hides were messy, over time we produced more elegant (and less smelly) results. Today we have garment-quality leather that's exceptionally soft, hardened leather for shoe soles, and thick, lustrous fur used in coats and other clothing.

The traditional leather and fur garments and other items of Native American tribes, particularly those of the Plains, are especially lovely. Samples traded (or taken) from tribespeople, as well as in contemporary use today, show a wide variety of patterns and sophisticated designs and symbolism. Cultures such as the Nez Perce, Comanche, Lakota, Cree, Cheyenne, and others worked with the hides of local animals. Deer, elk and buffalo hides, depending on geographic area, were particularly common. Quillwork, elk ivories, and beads were featured decoration for those who had access to them.[4]

The items that people wore in ceremonies were often animal-derived. Weasel skins, too small for most functional purposes, were incorporated into ritual wear as well as decorations by the Nez Perce and the Oglala.[5] A striking leather ceremonial shirt made by the Blackfeet was decorated not only with a bear claw, and a quillwork medallion depicting the Morning Star, but also locks of human hair.[6] Whole wolf and fox hides were worn by particular societies within the Oglala culture, and otter hides (among others) were used for sacred items and ritual purposes. Sentinels would wear whole raven hides on their heads to promote watchfulness.[7] And in numerous cultures worldwide, dancing in skins could be seen as a form of sympathetic magic to call prey animals for the hunt.[8]

One often overlooked use of animal parts is in the intricate textiles and weaving of tribes in the Andes. Several members of the camel family, most famously the llama, yield wool that is then turned into yarn. Clothing and adornments, dolls, and accents on flutes and other objects are all derived from the spinning and weaving of the wool.[9]

Sometimes the material an item was made of wasn't as important as other elements. A Crow shield depicts a grizzly bear's paw blocking bullets shot towards the bear's cubs. This motif represented the bear's power and protection, much valued in warfare. The rawhide that the shield was made of, on the other hand, held primarily practical rather than spiritual significance.

---

[4] Taylor, 1998 and Brown, 1997

[5] Landeen and Crow, 1997 and Brown, 1997

[6] Taylor, 1998

[7] Brown, 1997

[8] Evans and Clifton, 1997

[9] Davis and Fini, 1994

Additionally, a shirt from the Omaha that was worn by a person of high rank in the tribe also incorporated the strength of the bear through beadwork designs, but did not include any bear parts. A Lakota woman's dress made of a pair of deerskins had decorations representing turtles and buffalo for fertility, but again there were no parts from the latter two animals on the actual dress. [10]

An even more widespread traditional use for hides is the drum; hide drums are literally found worldwide. Usually, though not always, hairless rawhide, the drumskin is an example of careful engineering and refinement of processes over time. An improperly cured hide will have a subpar sound, and one that is not stretched properly will be similarly discordant.[11] The fact that cultures deemed to be technologically inferior by the more self-biased of Western minds could produce well-toned drums of many sorts, and with precise and deliberate variations, speaks well to their technical and aesthetic accomplishments. Yet time and innovation have brought us such varied designs as the West African djembe, the Irish bodhran (and numerous other frame drums found globally), and enormous drums such as Japanese taiko drums, powwow drums of various Native American tribes, and the lesser-known Lambeg drum of Ireland (often associated with North Ireland in particular).

Bones

Bones and their ilk have all served various purposes in humanity's history. Bones make great noisemakers, have been carved and cut up for beads and other adornments (and even early calendars, gambling devices, and tallying tools!), and bone shards have been made into arrow tips, bone awls, whistles, fish

---

[10] Taylor, 1998

[11] See Hart, 1990 for a superb, multi-faceted exploration of the history of drumming, particularly as a sacred act.

hooks, and other items. Antlers have served similar purposes, while hollow horns have been made into drinking vessels or reshaped into spoons and other utensils.[12] The Nez Perce were known for constructing quality bows. One style was particularly associated with the tribe, who developed it. A section of bighorn sheep horn was carefully reshaped, given a sinew backing, and the painstaking care in the process resulted in a high quality creation that was among the best of its kind.[13] Claws and teeth have largely been used as adornment, particularly in jewelry or accents on clothing.

The wing bone of an eagle, properly drilled, produces a distinctive whistle when blown and was used in the Sun Dance of the Oglala. Elk teeth were worn to promote longevity in the same culture, primarily because they were the most enduring part of the elk after death.[14] On a different continent, stag antlers were incorporated into English Morris dancing; these may have had prehistoric predecessors used by Mesolithic cultures.[15]

Sometimes animal parts could inspire myths. The skull bones of the sucker fish aren't completely fused together. After being cooked, the bones separate, displaying distinct shapes. They became fuel for tales about various beings in the Nez Perce mythos: "Some of the bones were named Grizzly's earring, Raven's socks, Stellar's jay, Softbasket woman monster, and Cricket packing her child".[16]

Bones have even played a part in divination. The knucklebones of sheep were thought to be the first casting bones.[17] Bone dice, in addition to being used for gambling, have also been utilized in foretelling. Scapulomancy involves taking the

---

[12] Feest, 1994

[13] Landeen and Crow, 1997

[14] Brown, 1997

[15] Jones and Clifton, 1997

[16] Landeen and Crow, 1997, p. 17

[17] O'Neill, 1994

scapula of an animal, placing it in a fire, and then reading the cracks in the bone that result; other bones could be used in similar ways.[18] A bone divination system derived from African tribal practices has been passed on to neopagans and others through Claire O'Neill's book, *The Oracle of the Bones*. While the book originally included a premanufactured casting cloth and plastic "bones", I easily found small bones that fit the bill for the Long Bone, Fat Bone, Small Bone and Broken Bone, and made a casting cloth out of a piece of deerskin I painted. If you happen across a copy of the book, with or without the original divination tools, I highly recommend it.

Feathers

Feathers are some of the best known animal parts used in cultural and spiritual rites, particularly indigenous American. Eagle feathers, particularly the black-tipped white tail feathers of the golden eagle, are especially famed for their importance to various Native American tribes. However, feathers have served as both adornment and sacred symbolism for countless millennia.

Practically speaking, feathers were the universal material for fletching arrows. And even in postindustrial cultures down is commonly used in coats, pillows and other items requiring the properties of "warm" and "soft". And while aesthetics aren't exactly practical, they're almost universally considered to be pretty, and so have been used for all sorts of decorative purposes in many cultures.

The eagle feather was quite possibly one of the most important spiritual items to the Oglala.[19] Along with eagle feathers, buzzard feathers also have significance to certain Native American cultures, particularly in the southwest U.S. and Mexico. The Ainu of Japan, on the other hand, favor blue jay feathers. Owl

---

[18] Whitcomb, 2008
[19] Brown, 1997

25

feathers have had associations (not surprisingly) with nighttime and the goings-on then. Peacock feathers are associated with Hera, and traditionally they were closely connected with the emperors of Japan and China.[20]

Sometimes the symbolism of the feather was of importance. In Egypt, the heart of the deceased was thought to be weighed against a feather (Ma'at). And in numerous cultures feathers symbolized the heavens, or the connection between the heavens and the earth.[21] This was sometimes embodied in actual feathers, such as a crane feather being a tool for better communication with the Divine in East Asia.[22]

Other Remains and Uses

It would be highly incorrect to say that all Native American (and other indigenous) cultures prominently featured animal parts in their creations. A large portion of Kwakiutl art was (and still is) composed primarily from plant-derived materials, especially wood. While animal parts may be used as an accent from time to time, they don't have nearly the prevalence seen in Plains tribes.[23] Considering it's easier to cut down a tree than shoot a deer, and trees are much more abundant in the Pacific Northwest than the Plains, this is not surprising.

Of course, indigenous American cultures don't have the monopoly on utilizing animal parts for ceremonial purposes. The compound retrieved by ethnobotanist Wade Davis that was supposedly the cause of Haitian zombies was found to contain a toxin derived from poisonous pufferfish. The compound induced a deeply sedated state in laboratory monkeys, which could

---

[20] Telesco and Hall, 2002
[21] Whitcomb, 2008
[22] Telesco and Hall, 2002
[23] Hawthorn 1994

explain the tales of shuffling, rudimentarily responsive zombies.[24]

Animal parts have also been used in medicine. Chinese traditional medicine in particular is notorious for utilizing animal parts, including those of highly endangered species such as tigers.[25] And while we don't have 2,000+ year old Celtic leather goods, we can guess that leather and other animal parts were utilized in everyday life as with numerous other pre-industrial cultures. When your resources are strictly limited to what's immediately available in Nature, animal parts necessarily are going to be a part of that.

Animal Parts and Modern Neopagans

The question of whether to utilize animal parts in modern neopagan spirituality is one that has no single definite answer. As with the population at large, pagans run the gamut from PETA members to hunters and all points in between. From my own experience, pagans are generally less weirded out by seeing others wearing animal skins, or bone pendants, or otherwise utilizing animal parts, in comparison to the population at large (in the U.S., anyway). While there are still pagans who see animal parts as gross, unethical, or otherwise distasteful, often they're considered to be under the broad (and not always accurate) umbrella of "shamanic".

The use of animal parts varies. Some people have them primarily as decoration, such as a skin on a shelf featuring various magical items. Others put them on altars as active representations of specific forces, such as totems or animal spirits, deities, powers of nature, etc. Still others house spirits; Yasmine Galenorn mentions an elk skull that has a spirit inside of it in her book *Totem Magic*.[26]

---

[24] Davis 1985
[25] Ghosh 2002
[26] Galenorn 2004

And then there are magical tools. These can range from Wicca-inspired general neopagan tools, like bone-handled athames and deerskin altar cloths, to neoshamanic totemic dance costumes made of skins, and even cattle horns converted to drinking horns for the offering of mead at heathen ceremonies such as blots. There are also fur and leather pouches to hold runes made of antler and bone, sacred jewelry with claws, teeth, and bone beads, and wall hangings of skin that represent any of a number of myths and mythological beings. (Much of this book will be dedicated to projects for making your own magical tools out of skins, bones and other animal parts.)

I do sometimes perceive animal parts as being valued more as fashion statements than for being remains of once-living beings. For example, there are many pagans wearing animal tails (especially fox, raccoon, and the like) at festivals—not as a part of ritual wear, but simply as part of one's outfit. This in and of itself isn't a bad thing. However, I do urge people to remember that these were once living beings, and should be honored as such. I wear a wolf tail at some events, but I do this not only for my own enjoyment, but so the tail and the spirit in it can have some time out and about. Additionally, it serves as a connection to Wolf, my primary totem.[27]

Etiquette

Just as with any magical tool, it's bad form to touch or pick up a skin or bone belonging to someone else without permission. There are any of a number of reasons for this. The owner may not want someone else's energy on the remains. The spirit within the skin or bone may not want to be bothered, or may only want to interact with the owner. The item may be in the process of being charged or in the middle of a ritual. And if the person is wearing

---

[27] Of course, this also raises similar questions about, say, leather footwear...

it, they may not be in an everyday state of consciousness.

A good example is skindancing, which is dancing in animal skins or other animal parts. I have been dancing with a full wolf skin since 2002 at various festivals. This is a sacred act that I share with other people, and it's also an opportunity for the wolf spirit in the skin to get a chance to dance with me. Being that the wolf skin is large, furry, and quite lovely to look at, there are people who find the prospect of "petting the wolf" to be irresistible. As with any trance dancer, it's a bad idea to touch me when I'm in the middle of a dance.[28] Jarring a person out of a trance can seriously unground hir, and be harmful to hir health on several levels. Additionally, if you touch someone who's aspecting a large predatory animal, don't be surprised if you get snarled at—a wolf is not a puppy dog. When I'm in full-blown trance, someone patting the top of my head is about the last thing I want!

Even if the setting is not a ritual, it's still not a good idea to touch someone else's ritual tools, animal or otherwise. If you see someone wearing a tail, don't run up to them and tug it. Would you do the same to the hem of someone's ritual robe if they were en route to the circle?

The other thing that I strongly recommend against is lecturing anyone wearing or carrying any sort of animal part (unless it's illegal). Chances are that person has good reasons for having it, and a guilt trip isn't very likely to make them agree with you. When I vend my at events, I've had people give me dirty looks, make snide comments, or even come up to me and say "Oh, the poor dead animals—why did you do that to them?" That's one of the best ways to get tossed right out of my booth. If you want to have a conversation like a grown adult, that's fine; I'll explain my animism if you want to hear it.

---

[28] It's also a bad idea to proposition me for a night in my tent, offer me alcohol, tell me bad jokes, start rattling off your life history—all things that have happened while I've been trance-dancing around drum circle fires!

In short, be respectful. Animal parts are controversial enough without bringing someone' spiritual beliefs and practices into question. If you must disagree with someone, be polite about it, and don't try to argue them into your way of thinking—would you like the same treatment? Better yet, just keep it to yourself if you can't stop at just asking polite questions that aren't veiled barbs. And consider that the people who have them have their reasons—which may include the following ones.

Reasons For Working With Animal Remains

I have a number of reasons for why I do this sort of work. Some of them are spiritual, though there are pragmatic reasons as well. Here are the biggest ones:

To Give the Spirits a Better "Afterlife"

This entire book is based on my belief that there are spirits in animal skins, bones, and the like, independent of the soul/spirit of the animal as an individual being. (I'll go into more depth about that in chapter three.) Because the spirits remain in the skins and bones until they decay, they're stuck with whatever fate their physical vessels have. It may not seem like a huge difference between hanging on the wall as a taxidermy mount, and hanging on the wall as an emblem of an animal totem. However, in my (subjective) experience, the skin spirits in taxidermy mounts are well aware of their "trophy" status. One of the most important reasons (if not the most important) I do skin spirit work is to give the spirits a more honorable afterlife than being a trophy or status symbol.

The lives that some of these animals may have led prior to death were pretty terrible. Living out your short life in a small cage barely big enough to turn around in isn't anyone's first choice of incarnations. Very few people in the fur, leather and food industries who work with animals are concerned with the psychological well-being of their charges beyond making sure that fur bearers don't tear out their hair from stress. Death often isn't much better, whether for farmed or hunted and trapped animals. While a well-aimed bullet can bring instant death, a bad shot can lead to injury and a slow, lingering, painful demise. Traps, of course, are painful, and even a few hours of excruciating pain is too much. Aquatic traps drown the animal, and anyone who's had a close call with drowning knows how terrifying that can be.

I can't make these things go away. I can help the spirits move on to something better. In chapter three I do describe a process I use to remove the spirit from the physical "container"; however, I've found that most spirits actually want to stay with their remains, and so I work to make the next part of their existences better than the previous. This is why much of what I make ends up being for ritual purposes, and I emphasize to people who buy them that they aren't just for show or the "shiny" factor.

To Make Connections With Spirits, Deities, and Other Entities

Primarily I integrate animal remains into work with animal totems. Skin dancing, as a part of my shamanic practice, involves not just calling on the spirit of the skin, but also the corresponding totem. Part of the development of my path and ritual form included creating songs and drumbeats for the skin spirits and their totems, and generally when I skin dance I also call on the totem of the animal I'm dancing with. While the skin spirit isn't the same being as the totem, the skin does help make a stronger connection to that totem.

However, it's entirely possible to use animal remains as ritual tools for connecting with beings other than totems. Deities and spirits who are associated with specific animals are a common choice. Just be sure that you acknowledge the spirits in

31

the remains themselves and get their permission for doing this sort of work.

To Avoid Waste

Much is made of the idea that Native American cultures made use of the entire animal from nose to tail. For example, to the Nez Perce "Wasting game of any kind was a serious offense against both the animals and nature and was believed to be punished with sickness or bad luck in hunting. The Nez Perce used every part of the animal they killed, partly out of respect to the animal and partly because of the utility of the products which could be obtained from them."[29] Similar things could probably be said of any culture that relies primarily on hunting and gathering, as well as agriculture, for survival. While in many such cultures there was respect for the animals, practicality was probably universal. However, the coexistence of respect and utility should not be underestimated, especially in this book.

Many animal remains that I work with have various chemicals in them that would make disposal problematic. Fur and leather are generally tanned with hazardous chemicals, and sometimes dyes as well. Bones, especially bone beads, may be painted or dyed. Feathers may also be dyed. Burying or burning these would release the residues *en masse* into the environment.

Additionally, I'm a big fan of the three green Rs--reuse, reduce, recycle. Thrift stores, online shops and other places have used fur coats, for example; while some of these may end up bought by people who wear them, others may end up in the landfill. I've obtained a number of the fur coats that I have from people who have given them to me because they don't know what else to do with them, and they figure I can make something neat out of them. If you're omnivorous and you buy meat with bones

---

[29] Landeen and Crow 1997, p. 13

in it, chances are the bones end up in the garbage. If you don't absolutely need to have the bones for your recipes, remove them prior to cooking, clean them (methods are available in chapter six), and work with them. It's quite possible to work with skin spirits from remains and castoffs of various sorts.

To Fulfill Aesthetic Desires

This may not be as noble as some other reasons, but I (and other people) simply like the look of fur, bones and other animal parts as artistic components. Sure, there are artificial reproductions made from various synthetics—faux fur, resin "bones", and so forth. However, nothing quite matches the look and texture of the real thing. Some people like ritual tools and other objects made from animal remains because of the "primitive", "tribal" or "shamanic" look to them. Others simply like the way bones are shaped, or the texture of certain types of fur.

Unfortunately, aesthetics have gotten a bad rap. For the most part in Western cultures, including the United States, aesthetics are the primary reason people use animal parts for clothing and other purposes. Fur coats are seen as a status symbol, while taxidermy mounts are meant to either give a room a more "rustic" look, or to show off the hunter's prowess. These aesthetic preferences are generally in absence of any regard for the animals themselves, spiritual or otherwise.

Part of the purpose of this book is to instill more than just an aesthetic appreciation of animal remains in artwork and rituals. However, I don't want people feeling guilty for simply liking the look of fur and bones. Instead, in addition to aesthetics, consciously consider other reason for working with animal parts, as well as the spirits in them, such as those I've given in this section. I perceive the problem not with aesthetics in and of themselves, but aesthetics without anything else to balance them out.

I've covered some of my reasons for working with skin spirits and animal parts. It's up to you to determine where your personal boundaries are in regards to this work. For now, though, let's move on to some more things to consider that may help you clarify your position: legal and ethical issues.

Chapter Two: Legal and Ethical Considerations

Before we go further, I'd like to discuss some issues that may not be as exciting as the prospect of skindancing, or creating a bone athame. Legal and ethical issues are incredibly important when working with animal parts, whether you're pagan or not, and so they get an entire chapter all to themselves. Don't skip this one!

Laws and Other Official Agreements Governing Trade in Animal Parts

Since I am primarily familiar with laws in the United States, I'll primarily be discussing those. However, if you live anywhere else, get in touch with the wildlife agencies at levels ranging from federal to local and find out what laws apply to you.

CITES

CITES, the Convention on International Trade in Endangered Species of Wild Fauna and Flora, applies to a number of nations that agreed to it. Stemming from discussion in the 1960s, CITES' development reached completion in 1975. Currently over 170 countries have agreed to abide by its terms. It is not a law in and of itself, but it provides a structure for each country to base its own laws on. While not all species that are protected under CITES are endangered, the agreement has gone a long way in helping cut down on illegal trade in animal parts (as well as live animals, and live and dead plants).[30]

CITES is divided into three appendices; animals are sorted

---

[30] CITES Secretariat 2008

into an appendix according to how threatened they are. Animals under each appendix have their own set of regulations on how they may or may not be traded, and by whom. From the CITES website:

Appendices I and II

Appendix I includes species threatened with extinction. Trade in specimens of these species is permitted only in exceptional circumstances.

Appendix II includes species not necessarily threatened with extinction, but in which trade must be controlled in order to avoid utilization incompatible with their survival.

The Conference of the Parties (CoP), which is the supreme decision-making body of the Convention and comprises all its member States, has agreed in Resolution Conf. 9.24 (Rev. CoP14) on a set of biological and trade criteria to help determine whether a species should be included in Appendices I or II. At each regular meeting of the CoP, Parties submit proposals based on those criteria to amend these two Appendices. Those amendment proposals are discussed and then submitted to a vote. The Convention also allows for amendments by a postal procedure between meetings of the CoP (see Article XV, paragraph 2, of the Convention), but this procedure is rarely used.

Appendix III

This Appendix contains species that are protected in at least one country, which has asked other CITES Parties for assistance in controlling the trade. Changes to Appendix III follow a distinct procedure from changes to Appendices I and II, as each Party's is entitled to make unilateral amendments to it.[31]

More details regarding what documents and other requirements

---

[31] CITES Secretariat 2008

are associated with each appendix may be found at http://www.cites.org/eng/disc/how.shtml. Additionally, you may search http://www.cites.org/eng/resources/species.html to find information on specific species protected under CITES regulations. Additional trade information on a country-by-country basis may be searched at http://www.unep-wcmc.org/isdb/extra/index.cfm. The CITES website, http://www.cites.org, has, of course, a wealth of information besides all this.

Please take note that animals killed prior to the ratification of CITES are not covered by it, according to Article VII. This means that if you have a vintage leopard fur coat or bear skin rug dating from before 1973, you don't have to worry about having CITES paperwork for it. Determining the age, of course, is another story. Some skins and so forth are obviously aged enough to be pre-CITES; others may definitely be family heirlooms. There may be some, though, that are indeterminate in age, and these you may want to be careful with or avoid altogether.

Migratory Bird Treaty Act and Migratory Birds Convention Act

The latter half of the 19th century saw numerous species of birds decimated in the United States. In addition to providing food, birds were a source of feathers for trendy plumed hats. The passenger pigeon, slaughtered thousands per hunt, was extinct in the wild by the turn of the century. An 1897 Michigan bill weakly attempted to temporarily stop hunting of the birds, but by that point there were so few left that a wild population was no longer viable, and less than a quarter century later the species was extinct, including in captivity.[32]

Three years after Michigan's proposed bill, in 1900, the Lacey Act was passed by the federal government. According to

---

[32] Department of Vertebrate Zoology 2001

the act, illegally hunted birds could not be transported across state lines if doing so were against the laws of the destination state. Unfortunately, the strength of the black market in animal remains overwhelmed the effectiveness of the Lacey Act. It was followed by the Weeks-McLean Law in 1913, which stated:

All wild geese, wild swans, brant, wild ducks, snipe, plover, woodcock, rail, wild pigeons, and all other migratory game and insectivorous birds which in their northern and southern migrations pass through or do not remain permanently the entire year within the borders of any State or Territory, shall hereafter be deemed to be within the custody and protection of the Government of the United States, and shall not be destroyed or taken contrary to regulations hereinafter provided therefor.[33]

Again, though, the law proved to be less than effective, but it provided a stepping stone for the Migratory Bird Treaty Act (MBTA) which was put into effect in 1918. The MBTA put full protection on the live specimens, eggs, nests, feather and other parts of all migratory bird species. This was in agreement with international treaties with four other countries; the "migratory" refers to species that are shared between Canada, Japan, Mexico, Russia, and the United States (meaning they are found in at least two of these countries at some point during the year).

A very high number of wild birds found in the United States are covered under the MBTA. This includes some that may surprise you. The blue, scrub and Stellar's jays, the American robin, and the Canada goose are just a few; no matter how common they may be, possessing their feathers, eggs, nests, or the birds themselves is illegal under the MBTA (with an exception that I'll discuss momentarily). You may find more information, including a complete list, at http://www.fws.gov/migratorybirds/intrnltr/mbta/mbtintro.html and its various links. Additional

---

[33] Fish and Wildlife Services 2002

information on the hunting and taking of migratory species may be found at http://www.access.gpo.gov/nara/cfr/waisidx_01/50cfr20_01.html.

Migratory game birds are a special exception in some cases. The feathers and other parts of *legally taken* migratory game birds (which includes various ducks, goose and other waterfowl, among others) may only be used for commercial purposes if they are for pillow, blanket and other stuffing. However, they may be possessed for any and all personal purposes that don't involve sale or barter. [34]

The Migratory Birds Convention Act (MBCA) is a similar agreement between the United States and Canada. Enacted in 1994, its predecessor, the Migratory Birds Convention, was signed into law way back in 1916. The MBCA regulates trade of birds that migrate between the two countries, to include all remains, eggs, nests, etc. More information is available at http://www.cws-scf.ec.gc.ca/enforce/law_1_e.cfm. (which also includes links to other Canadian laws). [35]

Bald (and Golden) Eagle Protection Act of 1940

The Bald Eagle Protection Act of 1940 specifically protects not only the bald eagle, but also the golden eagle. A 1994 provision allows for controlled distribution of eagle feathers to Native American tribes, and there are also provisions for research and exhibition purposes.[36] This is the infamous "eagle feather law" that often gets brought up in issues of religious rights, particularly related to the religious practices of various Native American cultures. Full text of the Act is available at http://permits.fws.gov/mbpermits/regulations/BGEPA.PDF.

On a side note, just in case you were curious as to where the

---

[34] United States Congress, 2001

[35] Environment Canada, 2005

[36] Fish and Wildlife Service, unknown date

feathers come from, the National Eagle Repository in Denver, Colorado is essentially a morgue for dead bald and golden eagles. This is where the requests for feathers and other eagle remains are sent and processed. It can take a while for a request to go through, since the number of birds received by the Repository is generally limited to about thirty a week, and there are thousands of pending requests.[37]

Marine Mammal Protection Act of 1972

In 1972, an act was passed that regulated the trade and protection of marine mammals such as whales and seals, as well as polar bears. In 1994, the Marine Mammal Protection Act (MMPA) was amended to allow for, among other provisions, more liberal hunting allowances for indigenous Alaskan subsistence fishing.[38] More information may be found at http://www.nmfs.noaa.gov/pr/laws/mmpa/, including full text of the MMPA. Additional information, including amendments not mentioned here, are at http://ipl.unm.edu/cwl/fedbook/mmpa.html.

Endangered Species Act of 1973

The Endangered Species Act (ESA) was enacted in 1973 in response to CITES and protects a wide variety of animals in the United States. It includes criteria for declaring a species of animal (or plant) threatened or endangered, details the nature of violations and penalties, and mentions its compatibility with the MMPA. While numerous amendments have been made to the ESA, the most notable occurred in 1978, 1982, 1988 and 2004; these dealt with everything from changing the criteria by which a species' status may be judged, to details on how to deal with an

---

[37] Draper, 2009
[38] NOAA OPR, unknown date

endangered species' habitat. Full text of the document is available at http://epw.senate.gov/esa73.pdf.[39] This law has been instrumental in preserving and aiding in the recovery of numerous species in the United States, though it has attracted controversy as well. Lobbyists representing ranchers and hunters who want to shoot wolves, for example, have pushed to weaken the ESA. In 2008, the northern Rockies wolf was officially taken off the ESA list of protected species, and hunting began shortly thereafter.[40] As of this writing several nonprofit organizations are working to reverse this decision.

The Wildlife and Countryside Act 1981

This law governs wildlife as well as wild plants in the United Kingdom. All birds are covered, and select other species as well. Multiple amendments have been made, including the Countryside and Rights of Way (CRoW) Act 2000 in England and Wales, as well the Nature Conservation (Scotland) Act 2004. The act details which animals may be hunted or otherwise killed, as well as those that are strictly off-limits. More information, including amendments and related laws, may be found at http://www.jncc.gov.uk/page-1377.[41]

Other Laws and Notes

These are just some of the legalities surrounding possession of animal parts. As I mentioned earlier, you'll want to research laws specific to your area, including state/etc., county, city, and so forth, as well as national/federal laws if you aren't in the United States. Something that may be permitted federally may be prohibited on a more local level. If you aren't sure what the

---

[39] United States Congress, 1973, et. al. and Fish and Wildlife Service, 2008
[40] Defenders of Wildlife, 2008; please also see the sidebar on this page for updates
[41] Joint Nature Conservation Committee, unknown

legalities are, contact the wildlife management branch of your local government.

Also, specifically regarding roadkill, many areas have restrictions against picking up roadkill. This is partly for public safety, particularly avoiding obstruction of the road as well as keeping human scavengers from becoming roadkill themselves. However, it wouldn't be impossible for an unethical person with a large, beat-up truck that has a heavy-duty grate on the front to deliberately hit a deer or other animal for unorthodox off-season "hunting", and then claim it was an accident. While one would hope that the potential for serious injury or death with this practice would prohibit it, there are people that stupid out there. I have heard of situations where game wardens allowed a person who did hit a deer to take it home—so if you do end up with this misfortune and want to make the best of it, ask permission from the law enforcement agents who show up on the scene. If they say no, then respect their decision.

I wouldn't be too concerned about scavenging skeletonized carcasses such as old roadkill. To be safe, I generally limit my bone scavenging to places where I'm less likely to get run over myself, such as the middle of a field. This, of course, does bring up trespassing laws, so if you're going scavenging on private property, make sure you have permission. Many public areas, such as state and federal park land, may have prohibitions on taking anything, whether animal or plant based, out of public land. Dead animals may be less of a concern than live, but you may want to ask a warden or other official on site about the regulations. While you're at it, ask if there are any scavenger or other possession permits that may allow you to legally collect roadkill.

If you hunt, obviously you need to be hunting in-season. Make sure you know when the proper seasons for taking a specific species are, as well as what tags you may need and how to properly report your kill. The same thing goes for fishing and trapping.

Online auctions, such as those on eBay.com, are a particularly sticky situation. While the company itself does its best to prevent prohibited items from being listed, they can't check to see if, for instance, that wolf skin you're looking at does in fact have its CITES information. It's very much a case of *caveat emptor*; if you see something listed on eBay or any other auction site that catches your eye, research the buyer and ask questions if you have to. There are a lot of reputable retailers who do use auctions as a form of extra income, but there are also those who sell questionable items.

One last thing to note: customs. When you're travelling internationally, it may be tempting to take home some nifty critter bit that you'd never find at home. Unless you're familiar with the protections on that animal, though, it's better to be safe. Some of the dealers in Appendix A can help get exotic animal parts; others you may simply have to wait for that once-in-a-lifetime shot at an antique shop or flea market. Trying to smuggle animal parts through customs, on the other hand? Not such a great idea.

Before You Start Complaining...

These laws may anger you. However, please keep in mind that they are there to protect animals from being driven to extinction by overhunting and other human activities. Don't try to get around them by claiming religious reasons; even Native American tribes have to deal with federal regulations to possess eagle feathers. Neopagan religions have even less power to become an exception to the rule than the tribes do. If you end up in court, chances are that trying to argue that having something illegal for spiritual reasons won't work.

A note on feathers: there is no way to tell the difference between a feather that was found on the ground, and one that was ripped out of the carcass of a bird that was shot illegally. I've heard all sorts of attempts to get around this, even people who go so far as to film their picking up a feather off the ground. (How would one prove that the feather wasn't pulled from a dead bird, then planted on the ground immediately before the film was taken?)

Granted, unless a fish and wildlife representative comes to your home or sees you carrying illegal parts at a festival, probably not much will happen. If you just happen to have a blue jay feather you found sitting on a shelf, it's not high on anyone's priority list. On the other hand, if you're proudly displaying a real eagle feather on your staff and someone sees it, don't be surprised if you get in trouble.

There may always be grey areas. For example, what if you happen to inherit an antique stuffed (taxidermy, not toy) owl of unknown origin? It's obviously old, but is it older than the Migratory Bird Treaty Act? Or what if you have a bear skin that doesn't have the official CITES paperwork, but does have the CITES number written on the underside of the skin? These will most likely be less of a concern than shooting hawks and falcons illegally to protect pet pigeons.[42]

No, it doesn't seem fair. After all, members of many Native American tribes can apply for permits to possess eagle feathers for spiritual use, and it can seem like religious discrimination because we can't do the same. However, there's a long precedent in indigenous use of eagle feathers; neopagan religions, while they might be inspired by older religions, are still new. Anyone can say they're a member of a religion that uses eagle feathers or other

---

[42] In 2007, the U.S. Fish and Wildlife Service carried out Operation High Roller, which resulted in the arrest of several roller pigeon enthusiasts being arrested for killing hawks and falcons. The raptors attack the pigeons, which are genetically bred to have mid-air seizures and "roll" towards the ground. This rolling makes them much easier for the raptors to catch. More details are available at http://www.fws.gov/news/newsreleases/showNews.cfm?newsId=BE935795-974F-4768-DE4A89664B1CFC29.

illegal parts, and if that were all it took, then people who trade in illegal animal parts on the black market could easily use that as an excuse.

When it comes down to it, the law is the final word; I'm not going to tell you what you should do, or report you if you go against the laws that have been enacted to protect the animals. I provide you this information so you can be aware of the legalities. You are responsible for your own actions and decisions.

Animal Rights Considerations

Because of the current cultural climates many pagans live in, working with animal parts may be considered controversial, to say the least. Advances in animal welfare laws and education on animal care in the past century or so have contributed to a drop in animal abuse. However, there's still disagreement as to how far the laws should go.

Some people argue that any use of animals is morally wrong. This can include not only leather, fur and other animal parts, but also eating meat (and sometimes other animal-based products such as cheese, eggs, gelatin, etc.), and even having pets (whether exotic, or your average domestic cat or dog). Others are more moderate in their stances; most people fall somewhere in the grey area between "animals exist for us to use" and "we should never use animals for anything".

It can be tough to navigate the information available on ethical issues. Even groups that purportedly work for the good of animals may be bogged down in controversy that overshadows the facts. For example, People for the Ethical Treatment of Animals (PETA) is a well-known, vocal group that argues against eating meat, wearing or using animal parts, animals in testing, and circuses, among others.[43] They have several satellite websites

---

[43] See http://www.peta.org for more details.

detailing specific issues. KentuckyFriedCruelty.com, for example, exposes the horrific conditions of factory farmed chickens, while PetSmartCruelty.com claims that pet store chain PetSmart treats animals sold in its stores poorly.[44] FurIsDead.com is dedicated to educating people about the reality of where fur comes from.[45]

At first their campaigns seem pretty straightforward. However, they aren't without at least their fair share (if not more) of criticism. One website, PETAKillsAnimals.com, goes to great length to expose PETA's history of euthanizing most of the animals given to them for rehoming.[46] A meeting of the U.S. Senate Committee on Environment and Public Works gave evidence that PETA had given money to the Earth Liberation Front, a group implicated in vandalism, harassment, and acts of violence.[47] Additionally, PETA's campaigns, which may include everything from naked women to pictures of dead, skinned animals, have come under attack from feminists who are angry about the exploitation of the women[48], and other animal rights activists who feel that PETA's shock tactics make the rest of the movement look "flaky"[49].

While most other animal rights and welfare groups aren't quite as far in the media spotlight as PETA, there are still ongoing debates over whether wolves should be reintroduced to their old ranges, even if livestock are there now; whether animals should be raised only for fur; whether laboratories should test medicines and procedures on animals; and whether lobbying groups are

---

[44] See http://www.kentuckyfriedcruelty.com and
http://www.petsmartcruelty.com for more details.

[45] See http://www.furisdead.com for more details.

[46]See http://petakillsanimals.com/ for more details. An article from 2005 may also be found at http://content.hamptonroads.com/story.cfm?story=93730&ran=57036

[47] See http://epw.senate.gov/hearing_statements.cfm?id=247266 for full text.

[48] See http://www.thefword.org.uk/blog/2008/03/fuck_you_peta and
http://www.blogher.com/can-you-be-feminist-and-support-petas-marketing-strategies for more details.

[49] See http://www.rickross.com/reference/animal/animal1.html for more details.

paying attention to all the potential issues, or just out to get money and political clout. It's a good idea to do your research on any organization you wish to contribute to in any way; while I feel confident about the ones listed in Appendix R, you may still want to find out the facts for yourself.

The same goes for ethical issues in general; regardless of what I or anyone else believes, in the end, the decisions you have regarding ethics are yours to make.

New or Secondhand?

People who feel uneasy about supporting the deaths of animals, especially for purposes other than food, may be consider secondhand animal parts instead of new ones. Whereas with new skins and other parts your money is going directly to the hunters, trappers or farmers who raised the animals whose remains you are purchasing, they can only be paid once. With the sale of secondhand parts, too, the demand for new ones is lessened.

Unfortunately, any demand for animal parts will continue the hunting, trapping and farming of animals for fur and other remains. And in a highly consumerist culture such as that found in the United States, selling one fur coat in good condition only to buy another brand new is perfectly acceptable. So while purchasing secondhand animal remains slows the demand somewhat, it doesn't stop it entirely.

However, if you're going to buy them regardless, my thought is that secondhand parts are better. While I don't exclusively use secondhand parts, I do incorporate them quite a bit. I have a lot of old fur coats, as well as some various bits of taxidermy. Additionally, while not truly secondhand, the skins of animal faces, tails and legs are generally castoffs from the fur industry, and would be thrown out if not used by crafters.

There are a few exceptions to this debate. Shed antlers from whitetails, elk, and other members of the deer family, as well as pronghorn horns, are gathered without any harm to the animals themselves. Additionally, if you happen to make yarn, a lovely yarn can be made from the shed fur of dogs. And technically wool can be gathered nonlethally, though the process of shearing can still be stressful for the sheep.

Hunted, Trapped or Farmed?

For most parts, though, some animal will have to die. Here's where, especially if you're going to buy new remains, you'll need to determine whether their origins are a concern to you. The two main ways in which wildlife is killed is through hunting or trapping; additionally, some species of furbearers may be farmed, and many domestic fowl provide feathers to the craft trade.

Hunting, if properly done, will produce the quickest death — a well-aimed arrow or bullet. My thought is that in this case the animal was able to live a life in the wild rather than a cage. On the other hand, "life in the wild" can be rough — many wild animals harbor parasites of one sort or another, and many die slow, linger deaths from starvation or disease. Additionally, a death by bullet or arrow is quicker than being chased by predators and pulled down by sharp teeth. With prey animals in particular, the meat is more likely to be eaten (though this is not universal, especially with trophy hunters who, for example, will shoot a buck and then only saw off the antlers, leaving the rest to rot).

Trapping, on the other hand, is more obviously inhumane. Many traps used don't kill the animal, but instead hold them in painful grips; animals have been known to chew off whatever appendage was caught. While some trappers may check their lines frequently, there's still a matter of at least hours where the animal will be in a complete panic and in pain, never mind the terror of not being able to escape when the trapper comes to make the kill. Some trappers may discard animals that weren't the species they were after, and traps don't discriminate between wildlife and outdoor roaming pets.[50]

Farming, in my opinion, is by far the worst of the three. In this case, animals live out their entire lives in small cages. Proponents of fur farms claim that their animals are well cared for, as a stressed animal will have a poor coat. The methods of killing the animals are supposed to be quick and as painless as possible.[51] On the other hand, many animal rights activists argue that the reality is much worse—that the animals routinely live in filth and squalor, and are killed in horrific ways.[52]

Should I Buy Remains of Endangered Species?

This is a tough decision for a lot of people. On the one hand, it's legal to procure the remains of wolves, provided they have the proper paperwork and weren't poached. And there are certain places, particularly in the northernmost portions of North America, where wolves are thriving. It's not quite the same situation as tigers, where every species is seriously threatened and trade in legal tiger parts is highly restricted (though sadly the black market is doing all too well). Is it okay to use the remains of a species that is endangered in some place if the animal was killed in a place where the population is healthy?

You may choose to only work with endangered parts that are legally taken from healthy populations, or that are secondhand, such as vintage coats. Or you might only work with non-endangered species' remains. Again, the decision is yours to make.

---

[50] Anonymous, 2009-A

[51] Montgomery, 2001 and Eggers, 2002

[52] Humane Society of the United States, 1998 and Friends of Animals, 2008

What About the Ethics of Roadkill?

I've heard the sentiment that it's more ethical to harvest bones and other parts from roadkill, since the death was accidental, not intentional. Well over a million deer alone are hit by cars in the U.S. every year, to say nothing of countless opossums, raccoons, skunks and other small animals.[53] However, cars pose one of the biggest threats to many endangered species as well. And unlike some hunters, very few drivers who hit an edible animal will harvest the meat—they're usually more concerned either with continuing on their way, or in the case of large animal collisions, with insurance companies and tow trucks right that very moment. In this respect, roadkill is more wasteful than factory farming, fur farms, or hunting and trapping.

We are the ones responsible for the deaths of numerous animals that end up as roadkill. It may be accidental, but our choices are responsible. When we insist on driving cars everywhere, when we chew up natural habitats with yet another cookie-cutter housing subdivision, and when we remove natural predators rather than learn how to live with them, we contribute to an environment where some species overpopulate and encounter busy roads more often. This, of course, gets into issues dealing with providing the resources for the growing population of the human animal, who in the Western world especially seems to require an awful lot per individual. However, that's a book or ten in and of itself. I'll just leave this topic with the assertion that roadkill isn't particularly ethical when you really look at it.

What's the Deal with Natural Deaths?

Over the years, I've had a number of people ask me if there's a reliable source of skins and bones from animals that died naturally. Generally these people are concerned with the ethics of

---

[53] Bell, 2008

farming and hunting, and want to feel better about what they're using. This is entirely understandable, as far as I'm concerned, and an animal that dies a natural death would seem to be a more ethical option than one that lived and died in horrific ways.

The fact of the matter is that most animals that die naturally end up biodegrading pretty quickly. There's not a company that specializes in sending out employees to canvass the woods and fields looking for critters that just kicked the bucket. An animal that dies naturally (if by that you mean died of disease, starvation, old age, and possibly attack by other animals) will quickly end up becoming food for scavengers, and then polished off by bacteria and other minute beings. The best you can find is bones, and even then it's not always easy to tell, for example, whether a deer died from being shot, or from starvation if there are no obvious breaks from bullets or arrows.

What about zoos? Generally speaking, when an animal in a zoo dies, the remains either end up used for research or cremated.[54] The legalities of dealing with a lot of the species in zoos can be pretty hairy, especially when the general public is involved, so it's easier just to dispose of the remains. I've known of a few zoo employees who had miscellaneous parts from work. However, don't go pestering them; they probably can't legally give you the remains anyway.

So about the best way for you to get parts from an animal that died naturally is to simply be there at death — which in most cases won't be possible. Most of us only ever witness the natural death of a pet, and there aren't many people who would be comfortable working with the remains of an animal they got to know that well (though there are exceptions). Shed antlers and molted fur and feathers are about as safe as it gets.

---

[54] Engber, 2006

Do Human Parts Count?

Ooooh. Here's a big, honking can of worms wrapped in a messy taboo. Not only do you have a very considerable amount of aversion to the handling of human remains in many cultures today, but you also have the debate as to whether humans are animals, or some higher order of being by virtue of our big brains/souls/blessing of the Divine/etc. Therefore, I'm going to address this *very* carefully.

I'll preface this by saying that I don't work with human bones. I have encountered them a couple of times as medical specimens, and the energy I get from them is something I don't really mesh with. We have a rather large, ugly complex about death that isn't present in (other) animals. While no animal probably enjoys dying, since (to our knowledge, anyway) we're the only animals consciously aware of our mortality, one of the driving forces in human cultures throughout history has dealt with either acknowledging or avoiding (or both!) death. In the United States, we don't really have a support system for approaching death with anything other than terror and avoidance, and you can see this running as a thread through our culture, often very subtly but powerfully.

Other cultures have not been as uncomfortable with human remains. A Tibetan drum known as a damaru was sometimes made with two human skulls.[55] Iron Age Celtic cultures featured a cult of the head, and while skulls were not the sole focus they were included in some practices.[56] In Haitian Vodou, Kenaz Filan (Houngan Coquille du Mer) states that "Bones are frequently found on shrines to Ghede and the dead. They are also used by many secret societies in rituals and wangas which are, well, secret. Without violating any oaths or confidences, I can say these have Kongolese roots and bear great similarity to practices found in

---

[55] Hart, 1990
[56] Heath, 1996

Brazilian Quimbanda and Cuban Reglas de Congo...I use legal remains for my work with the spirits: my Ghede Harvey drinks from a Tibetan half-skull Kapala, while one of our other spirits has a First Class Relic (a fragment of a saint's corpse, generally blood or a fragment of bone)."[57]

I would wager a guess that if you aren't already practicing within the parameters of a particular religious or magical path that utilizes human remains, and don't intend to join up, that you can at least begin your work with the remains in the same way as the other animal remains—speak with the spirits in them, and go from there. As I am speaking from a purely theoretical viewpoint other than my brief encounters with medical specimens, I can't say for sure what the difference would be in long-term work.

There are a few retailers that sell legally obtained human bones; the Bone Room (http://www.boneroom.com) is one notable example. Other than that, all I'll say is I won't touch your right to make a decision with a ten foot pole.

Minimizing Impact and Giving Back

I know I've dropped a lot of topics for consideration in your lap, some of which may be tough to deal with. However, I'd like to offer a few suggestions for ways to minimize your impact on the environment as well as on the animal kingdom:

--Buy legally. Poaching contributes a lot of stress on animal populations. Granted, hunting does, too, but hunting is at least generally regulated to prevent the decimation of populations. Legality is especially important for animals whose parts are only available on the black market, such as elephants, most big cats, and so forth. If you aren't certain about something, pass it by, no matter how good the deal may be.

---

[57] Kenaz Filan, personal communication, 18 August 2008

--Buy secondhand animal parts. Old fur coats and taxidermy mounts are good choices. However, even getting something like a tail or claw that another person bought new can help. It still won't reduce the impact to zero, but it's a better option than buying all new. Plus if you look for vintage remains, you can get things that are no longer available new, such as really old leopard skin coats or antique elephant ivory.

--Focus on found parts, especially those that came naturally from live animals. If you live in relatively rural areas, you may be able to find shed deer antlers, or tufts of hair. Feathers are another good choice, though again keep legalities in mind, such as the Migratory Bird Treaty Act in the U.S. The nonprofit wolf sanctuary, Mission: Wolf, sells bracelets made of fur shed from their wolves online at https://w82.webminders.com/missionwolf/store/asp/prodtype.asp?prodtype=38.

--Buy remains only from animals whose populations are healthy, or in the case of domestic animals, those that are ethically and sustainably raised. Or, alternately, only purchase remains from animals that were eaten as food, such as cowhide or chicken feathers. If you want to go the extra mile, get the feathers and hides from genuinely free-range animals, especially if you can verify that they were raised in open areas rather than barns or stockyards.

The other thing I want to address is giving back to the animals. While there's only so much we can do for those who are already dead, there's plenty we can do for the ones who still live and are yet to be born. While I elaborated on this at length in *DIY Totemism: Your Personal Guide to Animal Totems*, and don't want to repeat myself overmuch here, I'll hit some of the highlights.

One of the best things you can do is help nonprofit groups that aid wildlife and their habitat, and/or work towards better care and welfare of domestic animals. While there are organizations that seem to primarily exist for the purpose of political power and media attention, there are many more who are legitimately working to make the world a better place. I've included a selection of my choices in Appendix B; however, do your own research and determine who deserves your help the most. You can donate money to any group you like--they'll definitely appreciate it—or if it's a group local to you, volunteer some time. For example, you could see if a local wildlife shelter or animal rescue needs extra hands or resources. For myself, I donate a portion of all the money I make from my artwork to the Defenders of Wildlife and other nonprofits.

You don't have to help the exact species whose parts you work with, though it helps. However, if all you can do at this point is take good care of your pets and maybe volunteer some time at the animal shelter, it certainly counts. Of course, this is just on the mundane level of things. Any magic-worker can work magic for the purpose of helping animals. Again, I covered this in *DIY Totemism*, so I won't recycle material here. One important tip, though: focus on one specific issue, such as a potentially helpful law that needs a little help passing, or protection for a population of endangered animals threatened by poaching or pollution. I know some people like doing rituals to raise energy "to help all the animals in the world" or "wrap the world in white light". I find it's much more effective to be very focused so as to minimize dissipation of the energy directed. Think of it like shooting a gun—sure, a shotgun will get a wider spread, but a rifle will penetrate much more deeply.

The next chapter will go into more detail about the various rituals I do to aid skin spirits in my artwork; for now, considering legal and ethical issues, as well as everyday things you can do to help make animals' lives better, is a good start.

Chapter Three: Working With Skin Spirits

Here's where I get even more into my own unverified personal gnosis (UPG). Let me reiterate that this is very subjective material that is based primarily on my own experiences alone. If your experiences are different, respect that difference—don't assume either of us is automatically wrong or right, and for the love of whatever's important to you, don't take my word as concrete dogma!

So what, exactly, is a skin spirit? As far as I can tell, it isn't the full spirit (or soul) of the animal that once wore the body. Rather, it's a spiritual remnant that is soaked into the remains. One might think of it as the spirit of the body, rather than the spirit that inhabited the body for a time; or you might think of it as a localized haunt, a psychic impression left behind after death. It can be broken down along with the remains—the spirit of a full skin may be divided if the skin is cut into pieces. I believe that each cell has its own spirit, but when they're brought together they join as a collective to become what can be treated as a single entity. Normally when an animal dies the spirit dissipates as the body decays. However, many animal parts end up preserved, such as leather or fur, or kept in relative stasis, such as collections of bones and feathers. Therefore the spirits end up hanging around a lot longer than normal.

Skin spirits do have personality. Generally speaking, I've found that the more of the original animal that remains in one piece, the stronger the spirit is. I've also found that the "communicative" parts, the head, tail and limbs, tend to retain spirit more than the rest of the body, though there are exceptions. I speak to them through intuition and other nonvocal communication—I've yet to hear audible voices that I mistake for physical ones, which is probably a good sign! The conversations don't always happen in words; they may commonly occur in images, or even more raw feelings and sensations.

So what proof is there that the skin spirits aren't just my own projection of personality onto the energy that remains on the animal parts? Not much. The definition I provide, and in fact much of the animistic content of this book, is based on my subjective perceptions and the beliefs I draw from them. What's most important to me, though, is that spiritually and magically my belief in the existence of skin spirits has function and purpose. It not only allows me more connection with my spiritual path, but it also encourages me to have more consideration for beings other than myself—even if they aren't alive. It has helped to give me an artistic practice that has improved my life in many ways, and aided me in developing beliefs that give me a firmer understanding of the world around me. And even if it all is in my head, it brings me greater spiritual fulfillment; this, to me, is reason enough to allow myself this belief.[58]

Finding Skin Spirits to Work With

In the last chapter, and in the upcoming chapters on individual animal remains, I discuss where to go to find skins, bones and so forth. However, how do you know what you should get? Here are a few potential starting points:

--Do you have a specific species you have a connection to? Would you feel more comfortable working with a species you're already familiar with in some way, such as through a totem or other animal guide?

--Do you already have something to work with, perhaps an

---

[58] Some might argue that the potential harm done to animals invalidates my belief; I'll discuss this more in chapter Y.

inherited fur coat, or an antler found in the woods?

--Do you feel a calling towards a particular part of the body? Would you like to start with a tail, or maybe a claw, or some feathers?

--What about your ethical and legal boundaries—do these affect your choices? How about financial limitations, or accessibility?

Beyond that, what about the individual skin spirits themselves? If you're ordering online, you'll probably have limited exposure to the spirits. However, if you have a chance to shop in person, you'll be able to "talk" with the spirits as you browse. Sometimes it may be very obvious that a spirit wants to go home with you. I've had situations where the call was "loud" enough that other magically-inclined people with me could hear it as well as I could! Other times, though, I don't really get a chance to have a good conversation until I've gotten the spirit home and had time to really sit down with hir.

Just as a clarification, I am not of course referring to physical speech. Call it intuition, telepathy, or whatever term/categorization you like—technically you could even call it psychometry, since I use physical touch to "read" the energy of the spirit. It comes to me in sensations and images more than words, though I'll often "translate" it into words to better get a handle on what's being communicated. The right brain gets it—the left brain needs a little help.

If you've spoken with spirits before, either those embodied in vessels of various sorts or not, you may find speaking with the skin spirits to be a familiar thing (no pun intended, I promise!). If you haven't though, here's a simple method. Go someplace where you won't be disturbed for at least a half an hour, longer if you think you'll need it. Sit with the remains in your lap and under your hands. Quiet your mind and slow your breathing. Focus on the feeling, the energy, of the spirit in the remains. (If you've never even done energy work, I'm not a good person to try to explain exactly what it feels like, especially since different people get different impressions. All I can really say is once you sense it, it becomes distinct pretty quickly.) Then open yourself to the spirit, and see what pops into your mind. This can take some practice, because as with any form of meditation our brains like to distract us from being quiet. However, if you "hear" a "voice" that isn't yours, pay attention. You will want to practice this several times over time, because just because an unfamiliar voice speaks doesn't mean that it's true, or even that it isn't just in your own head.[59] Once you get more experience, though, you'll be able to tell what's internal and what isn't, and even be able to determine who's talking without physical contact. It helps if you have more than one skin spirit to work with so you can tell both similarities and differences.

Once you've got the hang of this sort of communication, take some time to get to know the spirits you're working with. Ask them about their lives — and their deaths, if they're comfortable talking about that. Discuss your own situation and intent, too, and see what they think of it. If the spirits have specific things they'd like their remains to be made into, listen to them and do the best you can to make that happen. If a skin spirit rejects your ideas, respect hir wishes.

After the Introductions Are Through

So now what do you do? Read on for some basic ideas. I'll be elaborating on them in later chapters, but this will give you some context for now.

---

[59] It could be said that it's all in our heads, and that skin spirits are just projections of the psyche. For the purposes of both this book and my spiritual/magical path, I assume that they are independent beings. Your mileage may vary.

Skin Spirits as Themselves

Sometimes you don't really need to do anything with the remains except let them be themselves. Many pagans simply have skins and bones that they have in their ritual areas; others may wear a skin as part of ritual regalia, draped over a shoulder or a smaller skin hung from a belt. If a skin spirit seems perfectly happy in hir present form, don't fix what isn't broken—one of the main purposes of skin spirit work, in my opinion, is making the spirits happy. I have a whole collection of skulls who are content to hang out on the walls of my ritual room, apart from the others who end up as various ritual tools and artwork.

Skin Spirits as Vessels

Besides holding the spirit of the animal that once wore the skin/bone/etc., remains can also be incorporated into vessels for housing other spirits. *It is very important that you get the permission of the skin spirit before introducing others.* In some cases the skin spirit may refuse; in others, s/he may ask to be removed from the remains (more on that later in the chapter). There are cases, though, where a new spirit may simply invite hirself in, whether the skin spirit wanted hir or not.

You may want to do a formal ritual to invite the new spirit in. Depending on the situation, you might also decorate the remains, or make them part of a more elaborate structure. Even if the original skin spirit agrees to sharing, or wishes to depart, I find it good practice to honor that skin spirit in some way in the decoration or construction of the final vessel.

Ritual Tools/Helpers

Skin spirits may become more active parts of your magical practice through being incorporated into ritual tools. (There'll be plenty of ideas on what to create in the chapters to come.) As with the spirit vessels, you'll want to get the skin spirit's permission to be made into a particular item. Once you've created the ritual tool, make sure that you greet the skin spirit(s) (if they're still there) when you use it, rather than treating it as an inanimate object with no spirit in it.

Acknowledging that spirit can be very helpful in magical practice. Rather than evoking external spirits, you may wish to simply ask for the skin spirit's help, and let the ritual tool be a channel for hir aid. Something else to consider is whether there may be conflict between the skin spirit and any other spirit evoked. I've not had it happen, but it's always a possibility; I tend to work mostly with animal spirits of various sorts, so there's plenty of common ground.

Art for Art's Sake

Sometimes it's enough just to make something that's aesthetically pleasing, with no practical purpose beyond decoration. Unless you remove the spirit from what you've created, though, it's a good idea to treat the artwork as a spirit vessel. Even if the spirit is content to sit and look pretty, acknowledgement goes a long way. I find in my own home that skin spirits housed in artwork tend to become guardian spirits of wherever they're placed and interact with the rest of the house spirits on their own.

Purification and Other Rituals

I covered some purification rituals in *Fang and Fur, Blood and Bone*, so if you've read that book, some of this may be familiar to you. There are a number of rituals that I use in the process of turning animal remains into ritual tools, artwork, etc. You are welcome to use or change these, or create new ones as you see fit.

Before I do any sort of cutting or other "deliberate damage" to animal remains, I do a sort of "spiritual anesthesia". Now, I know full well that there aren't any functioning nerves left, and no brain to connect them to. However, I've observed distress in spirits whose remains were being cut and stitched. It's not a physical pain, but it is a discomfort. So I developed a rite to address this.

First, I lay out the skin/etc. on the floor before me (if you work at a table, use the table). I make sure that if it's a skin, it's laid out flat. Next, I hold my hands about a foot above the remains, and run them from one end to the other, smoothing the spirit's energy out. I continue this several times, lowering my hands more each time and pushing the energy down. On the last pass, my hands brush over the surface of the remains. I then lift my hands up and then press them straight down onto the remains. After my physical hands stop at the skin/etc., my spiritual hands continue downward, carrying the spirit in them. I lull the spirit to sleep and leave hir in a spiritual cave below me to rest. Once I'm finished with the project, I'll then call the spirit back up to see the results.

Next will be the purification rite. I primarily use this for remains made into ritual tools and artwork for others, but you can use it for any skin spirits. First, I purify the physical remains with a smudge of sagebrush; you can use whatever sort of smudge you like. I don't recommend water because it can damage some remains, and fire can singe or burn. Smudging seems to do a good job of energetic purification.

I also do a meditation with the skin spirits in the project I'm purifying. I'll ask each one to tell me about hir life and death, whatever s/he would like me to know. I also will visualize the parts of me that correspond to the spirits' remains — if I'm holding leather, I look at my own skin and imagine what it might be as leather, and imagine what the leather was like as living skin. This reminds me that these weren't just textiles made in a factory — they were once living beings, just like me.

Finally, I make an offering to the totems that watch over the spirits. I have a small leather pouch for each of the species whose remains I commonly use, and another one for the world which includes all other animals. I'll give a certain number of small drilled stones or beads for each remain used. Once a pouch is completed, I make the stones and beads into a necklace which I then give to a person who works with that species' energy, either with the totem, or spirits, or even the physical animals.

Removing Spirits

While in most cases the skin spirits I've worked with have opted to stay in their remains, occasionally they've chosen to leave, or in a couple of extraordinary cases, I've had to remove them for other reasons. I don't recommend doing this unless it's requested or necessary; it's highly disrespectful to evict a skin spirit from hir own remains, especially for selfish purposes.

First, lay the remains out as you would for purification. Then reach down and simply "pick up" the spirit and place hir next to the remains. I usually see myself as grasping the head of the spirit, right behind the curve of the lower jaw; I'm not sure why this is — it just always seemed to be the best place to do so. I give the skin spirit time to adjust. Either s/he'll opt to stay with me and be a part of the household spirits, or s/he'll go off to wherever s/he wants to go now that s/he's no longer attached to hir remains. I've never had trouble with this process, though I got a lot of protestation from the spirits I forcibly removed.

It is possible to place the spirit into a new vessel, either another animal part or a non-animal-based vessel. In the former case, of course, get the permission of the resident skin spirit if s/he's still there. Otherwise, you can place the spirit directly into the vessel, or allow hir to take up residence at hir own pace.

Why Leaving Skins/etc. as Whole as Possible Is Better

As mentioned earlier, skin spirits may be composed of the spirits of individual cells. When you cut a piece of leather in half, for example, you end up with two skin spirits, not one living in two vessels. The smaller the piece and the less connected to the whole animal, the weaker the spirit is. I tend to not cut up larger remains into smaller ones if I receive them whole because I want to preserve as much of the spirit as possible.

This practice ultimately gives me more to work with. One stronger spirit seems to be more effective in magic than many weaker ones. Additionally, it seems to make the spirits happier. While you can create somewhat of an amalgamated energy when you stitch two different skins together, for example, you don't get one single animal spirit. You may have the energy of the creation, but the individual skin spirits are also discernible in most cases. Also, on that note, if you do have two skin spirits that seem opposed to being brought together, respect their wishes and find something else to do with them. Linking two antagonistic spirits together is sure to bring nothing but trouble in the long run.

Other Peoples' Creations

If you aren't an artist yourself, or if you otherwise come across something that someone else made from animal parts, you can still work with the skin spirits. Depending on how the creation was made and who made it, the skin spirits may be unhappy, or they may be perfectly content. In the former case, ask the spirits why they're displeased. They may simply not have had anyone to talk to about their lives/deaths, or they may have felt like they were handled in a disrespectful manner when being incorporated into someone's work.

While most of the time you should be able to calm the spirits down and explain to them how the current form their remains take will be treated in a respectful manner, occasionally you may get spirits that still insist on having the artwork/tool disassembled, and the remains either left alone or made into something different. If you have artistic tendencies, this may not be so intimidating; however, if you haven't got an artsy bone in your body you may consider either A) trying to convince the spirits to keep their vessel as-is, or B) commissioning an artist to do a bit of custom work for you.

For example, one time I bought a "medicine shield" secondhand at a flea market that had a fox skull surrounded by chicken feathers. For whatever reason, the spirit in the skull did not like being surrounded by the feathers, which led to a rather disharmonious piece overall. After saying a prayer to the original, anonymous artisan to thank them for their work, I took the shield apart. The fox skull has preferred to hang out in my ritual room ever since.

Faux Skin and Other Alternatives

You may be opposed to the idea of working with animal parts in magic; or you might not be able to afford a part or it may be illegal to buy or possess, depending on species and location. Or you might be working with an animal that's either extinct, fantastic, or otherwise not physically found on this plane of reality. This doesn't mean you can't do this sort of magical work, such skindancing—it just means that you need to find a suitable substitute. Fortunately there are plenty of options[60].

Fake fur is available at just about any craft store. Some of it looks quite realistic, though you can also get it in just about any crazy color you can think of, as well as various hair lengths and textures (I've never heard of anyone wanting to dance as a bright pink yak, but the appropriate faux fur is out there!). Or, if you prefer, you can buy fabric that has pictures of the animal on it; wolves, bears and other Big, Impressive North American Birds and Mammals (BINABM) are quite common. If you're dancing a reptile there's fake snakeskin and gator-print vinyl available.

---

[60] Throughout this chapter I will refer to real fur and substitutes as skins in a general manner; the function is essentially the same.

Feathers are a bit tougher, though you could get plain fabric and either stitch feathers to it[61] or paint them on.

I recommend creating a pelt that fits you, even if it's larger than the actual animal. After all, a rabbit skin, even from a domestic rabbit, averages about 6" x 12", which is about enough to cover a decent-sized bald spot. You may want something that covers a bit more to help add to the illusion that you actually have sprouted fur, feathers, scales, etc. all over your body.

You don't have to create an entire pelt. As with real fur, you can construct a simple set of ears and a tail, or wings and beak— whatever you see fit. This may actually be more comfortable, as in my experience faux fur actually traps heat even better than real fur. Additionally this may be simpler and cheaper, and certainly results in a more portable "pelt".

You can also buy faux fur coats rather than new fabric if you want to be more environmentally conscious. Even if you extol the virtues of faux, keep in mind that the plastic used to create fake fur and other synthetic fabrics is largely petroleum-based, and there are additional chemical residues as a result of the process. At least by using secondhand materials you're reducing the amount of consumption of new resources.

And fake fur isn't your only option. As I've mentioned elsewhere, there are artificial reproductions of claws, talons, and even bones available for purchase. The concept is still the same— substitution. Something as simple as a pendant or other piece of jewelry, or a t-shirt, or other adornment that has the image of the animal will work in a pinch. You could even bless a particular set of body paints and imbue them with the spirit of the animal. Basically what you want is something that will serve as a physical vessel for the animal spirit you want to work with to reside in since there are no physical remains. Which brings me to the next

---

[61] Be aware that most of the feathers that are sold for craft use come from birds that were killed for other purposes such as food, rather than being naturally shed.

section...

It's Alive! (Well, Sort Of ...)

With a real animal part, there's already a resident animal spirit of sorts. However, when you're working with plastic or fabric or metal or other non-animal materials, you're starting from scratch. This, of course, necessitates finding an animal spirit who's willing to work with you to take up residence in your substitute skin.

Finding any sort of spirit guide isn't as easy as opening up the Yellow Pages and hunting through the directory. However, the aforementioned totemic meditation is quite sufficient for seeking individual guides. Alternately, you may contact the totem that watches over the species you want to work with and ask hir to connect you with a spirit; the totem may even give you a piece of hirself (which to some people is what any animal spirit, in a body or not, really is).

You can even construct an animal on the astral plane. In *Fang and Fur* I dedicated a chapter to creating new species on the astral using the concept of servitors (magical thought forms).[62] Again, you may contact the totem for help with this project. Basically, create a servitor of the species of animal you want to work with, and use your faux pelt/pendant/etc. as hir physical representation.

This brings me to an odd little tangent. I know that occasionally pagans have used the actual skin of one animal to represent or embody the spirit of another. For example, if you're working with a leopard spirit, but all you have is a bit of bobcat fur, can you use that fur to house the leopard? Well, that all depends on the individual situation. While in my experience most spirits in skins and other animal parts are content to stay where

---

[62] If you're completely new to the idea of creating servitors, a wonderful step-by-step guide to doing so is *Creating Magical Entities*, cowritten by Taylor Ellwood, Amanda Wagener and David Cunningham.

they are, occasionally I've run across ones who have wanted to move on from their remains, in which case I lift the spirit up and place hir beside the pelt, as well as offer hir the run of my home as long as s/he wishes.

However, in this situation suppose the bobcat is quite cozy in that piece of fur. Rather than forcibly removing the original inhabitant, try asking if s/he's willing to share with the leopard and let the skin have double duty. Conversely, you might also consider dancing with Bobcat instead, since you already have a good connection available to you. If worst comes to worst, finding leopard-print fabric is almost frighteningly easy.

Now that you've gotten a heaping helping of theory, let's get on to what many of you may consider "the good stuff" — the practical, hands-on part of the book!

Chapter Four: A Brief Chapter on Tools

There are numerous tools and supplies that you can use for the crafty exercises I'll have in the next few chapters (the tools available just for leatherworking is mind-boggling). However, I'd like to discuss the tools that I personally use most commonly in my artwork, as well as a few others you may find useful. I'll try and keep this simple, though if you really want to get specialized tools beyond these there are options with some of the businesses in Appendix A.

Scissors: These will come in handy numerous times for cutting everything from thread and wire to leather. You're perfectly welcome to buy an expensive pair of scissors if you like. However, I usually pick up a cheap pair of kitchen shears; they work just as well for cutting all but the thickest of leathers. Sometimes I'll retire an old pair to other uses, like cutting paper; other times I'll take them to a knife shop to be resharpened.

Craft blade: The most popular type is the Exacto ™ knife, a metal handle with a slit at the top for inserting individual blades. However, I've also used a type of small utility/box knife found in the hardware section that has a segmented blade. Whenever the edge gets too dull, snap off the segment to reveal a fresh edge.

Glue: Again, you can pick up all sorts of fancy craft glues, but I find that regular white glue works well for just about everything I need. If I need something a little heavier duty, I'll pick up Aleene's Tacky Glue. For quick fixes, especially bones that may be difficult to clamp together, I have a small bottle of super glue. And for really strong bonds, I use J-B Weld, a steel-epoxy mixture.[63] I've never had much luck with hot glue. With fur and leather, the layers of hide directly attached to the glue can peel off causing detachment, and hot glue doesn't, in my experience, have enough strength to hold heavier objects like bones, nor does it last over time on animal parts in general. It's good for synthetic plants and the like, but I strongly recommend having the patience for white glue to dry. Additionally, there are some projects you don't want to rely only on glue for. For example, if you were to make an X out of two rib bones, you could spot-glue with super glue, but then you'd want to tightly bind the bones together with cord or leather lacing. Glue is a good temporary fix, but most times you'll want to back it up with something else.

Needles: Personally, because I tend to use lighter-weight garment leathers such as deerskin, I prefer glover's needles, with a sharp three-sided point which will go right through the leather. My favorite needles are John James size 1 glover's needles, which can be bought in packs of 25 for a reasonable price. They have a large enough eye for the type of thread I use (discussed below) and are durable besides. However, other people like using a simple awl and mallet to punch holes in hides, especially heavier leathers, then using a blunt-tipped leather needle for the actual stitching. It's time-consuming, but you can use heavier threads than with glover's needles. There are also specialized awls that stitch as you punch the holes; I've not used them, but people I know who have swear by them. Finally, if you use a sewing machine, there are specialized needles and feet for stitching hides.

Thread: I'm not talking about sewing thread here. Instead, I tend to use artificial sinew, and waxed linen cord. Both of these can be split down to several threads that will fit in glover's needles

---

[63] Because of the chemical composition of this product, you'll want to make very sure that if you get any on your skin you wash it off immediately.

better, though the sinew tends to be stronger. Both come in a variety of colors, though sinew tends to have more choices. Usually I just go with "natural"-colored sinew. You can get real deer sinews, though these are expensive and are limited in length. However if you're going for 100% natural (especially animal-based), that's the best choice; a few strands of horse hair can also make a good, if somewhat difficult to work with, thread. If you're working with a machine, make sure you get a heavier-duty thread, since some leathers can be pretty heavy. Do be aware, too, that there will always be leathers and other materials too heavy for you to stitch with a machine.

Paint: For painting on leather and bone, I haven't found anything that beats acrylics. They're inexpensive, and they take to the natural surfaces very well. Oils blend better because they take longer to dry than acrylics, but I don't like their texture as much. There are special paints made for leather, but I've had enough good experiences with acrylics to not want to pay more. As for paint brushes, I tend to just pick up the multi-packs to save money, though again if you want to use higher quality brushes you're more than welcome. Also, make sure you have a cup for paint water to rinse brushes if you're using acrylics or other water-soluble paints, or paint thinner if using oils.

Mod Podge and Acrylic Sealer: You will want to seal anything you've painted to help prevent chipping and other damage. Acrylic sealer spray tends to work the best on bones and other "solid" items—make sure you use it outdoors! I do like Mod Podge, though, for paint on leather, because I can apply it with a paintbrush only to the painted areas if I want the rest of the leather to stay its original color and texture. Be aware that if you use Mod Podge on bones/etc., it can get tacky in the heat, especially if you use multiple layers. I generally reserve it for things where I need sealant only on very specific areas that the acrylic spray is too widely applied for.

Ruler: If you want to be precise about measurements, a ruler is a must. It's also very helpful for tracing and cutting straight edges. I have a nice metal one that was left by a former roommate, but any ruler will work. I recommend one at least a foot long.

Leather Punch: If you want to use leather lacing to stitch things together, or want nice, neat holes for threading drawstrings and the like, a leather punch is quite handy. It consists of a squeezable two-part handle; one part has a wheel of different-sized punches on it, and the other has a flat piece of metal to push the punch against. Simply put the leather between these two parts, and squeeeeeze the handle, and you now have a perfect circle punched through! I usually only punch one layer of leather at a time, but I also don't have particularly strong hands. You can also use a regular awl, but the hole will be smaller and not as neat since you're pushing the leather out of the way, instead of taking out a piece entirely as with the leather punch.

Jewelry/Beading Wire and Findings: If you plan on making jewelry, you'll want a good, strong wire for it. I dislike fishing line, partly because of the look, and also because a knot that isn't tight enough can come undone. There are special beading cords out there, though I prefer metal wire, such as tiger tail, since it doesn't fray (though it can snap under too much weight). If you use wire you'll need crimp beads or similar findings to finish off the ends, and also clasps and jump rings. Many craft stores will have beginner's pack of jewelry supplies; additionally, there are numerous books on creating jewelry--see Appendix C for suggestions.

Pliers: The best pliers will probably be jeweler's or small needle nose pliers. They're good for pulling glovers' needles through thick hides, holding items when you don't want your fingers too close to a carving tool or other potentially hazardous thing, and, of course, making jewelry.

Dremel: The Dremel is a wonderful thing. It's sort of like a small drill, except you can put all manner of things on the end besides different sizes of drill bits — cutting bits, carving bits, sanders, and other fun things that are indispensable to many artists. If you want to do any sort of work with bone and horn and antlers, you'll want a Dremel. I prefer the one with the cord, because I hate having to recharge the battery on the cordless one in the middle of a project. However, you may like the cordless because, well, there's no cord to get in your way. You can get a basic Dremel starter pack at most hardware stores, and then add bits as needed. I do strongly recommend making sure that you have a set of different sized drill bits made for the Dremel, as well as a cutting wheel. There are packets of cutting wheels that are meant for cutting metal; you can use them on bone, but they shatter easily if you don't hold the Dremel steadily. There's also what amounts to a miniature saw blade, but it'll cut through your bone as easily as a deer bone, so you'll want to be incredibly careful with it.

Safety Gear: If you're going to be using a Dremel at all, you'll want to have a good pair of goggles and a face mask (like the kind that doctors wear in surgery, available in any hardware store). The goggles, of course, will protect your eyes. The face mask will keep out bone dust, which can cause respiratory issues over time. Buy a package of face masks and replace them every few weeks if you do a lot of work. And if you have the saw blade for the Dremel, you should seriously consider investing in a pair of Kevlar gloves.

Cutting Board: Besides being a good surface for cutting things on (so as to save your table, counters, floor, etc.), the cutting board can also be very useful in stitching. If you're using glover's needles and you're having a tough time getting the needle through a piece of hide, carefully brace the needle's eye against the board and push the leather down the needle. Or, if you're using an awl, the board can easily take the damage when the awl comes out the other side of the hide.

If you've never done a particular type of project before, look for kits to start with. Use them to get an idea of how the item is put together and how the tools work; then try making one from scratch when you feel comfortable. For items such as clothing, you may want to work with patterns, especially if you're making items for bodies other than of those around you. In the event that someone far away needs something, you can go by the sizing on the pattern mixed with the person's measurements.

Also, it's helpful to have more than one of the tools you use the most, such as scissors or glue. My art room tends to be messy, and things like to migrate away from where I left them, so having backup can let me work on a project that I'm in the mood to work on *right this moment.* I can always go looking for the lost items later, or wait until they show up again of their own accord (or the next time I clean up the room).

Chapter Five: Fur and Leather

What's a Hide *Fur*, Anyway?

A hide, of course, is skin, and therefore on a living animal serves many of the same purposes across species, to include humans. It's a waterproof protective organ, selectively permeable, that in mammals hosts hair, in birds feathers, and in reptiles and most fish, scales. It defends the rest of the body against bacteria and other germs, as well as potential causes of injury. It's the wrapper for all vertebrates.

Skin is full of sensitive nerves which compose the sense of touch. It's one of the first ways vertebrates connect with the environment around them and the denizens thereof. Through skin a vertebrate can perceive temperature, pain and pleasure, and other sensations. Touch is also an important vehicle of communication, from anger to affection and all points in between.

It also has features that evolve in specific species to reflect their environs and other factors affecting their health. The oils produced by the skin, as well as the pores themselves, may help with either shedding or retaining water, for example. For some species, particularly of amphibian, skin may actually be a respiratory organ. Coloration may also help with camouflage or communication, such as in mating or territory displays.[64]

Where to Get Fur and Leather

-- Wholesalers and retailers, including those in Appendix A
--Secondhand fur coats, leather clothing and taxidermy mounts

---

[64] Anonymous, 2009. Sadly, in humans the amount of melanin in one's skin is all too often a bone of contention, and has been the source of entirely too much violence and persecution.

from thrift stores, flea markets, yard sales, etc.
--For the truly intrepid: hunting, scavenging fresh roadkill, frozen snake food (rats, rabbits, etc.)

Physical Care of Fur and Leather

Hides that have been tanned well and are cared for can last for decades. Leather has a tendency to hold up better than most furs, though part of that is because typically the hides for leather are thicker, especially when you compare, say, steerhide with rabbit fur. With attention, though, you can keep skins in good condition for quite some time.

One of the biggest threats to leather and fur is drying out. Leather may often have a coating on it to help prevent this, and so isn't as vulnerable. However, both leather and fur should be treated periodically to keep them hydrated. I tend to prefer mink oil in cream form, rather than the messier liquid, though saddle soap and neatsfoot oil are also options. Many treatments may leave leather darker in color, so if you have a hide whose color you're particularly attached to, you may want to test a small inconspicuous portion of it with the treatment first. With leather you want to work the treatment into the smooth side, while with fur you'll give attention to the hairless side.

I take an old, soft rag and use it to apply the treatment; I also may simply use my fingers. I then gently work it into the hide, especially older ones that may be prone to tearing. Use enough that the hide is rehydrated, but not so much that it stays greasy. You might take a clean rag to wipe up any excess. Make sure to get all the nooks and crannies, especially if you're working with hides with feet still attached. There's no set time interval for treating hides; if the skin starts to dry out, or if it becomes less supple, it may need attention.

I usually end up treating furs a lot more often than leather, every couple of years for older ones, and a little longer in between for newer ones. Leather usually doesn't need treatment that long unless you have it out in the sun or heat a lot. If the leather begins to crack (not just crease) or looks noticeably faded, it probably needs oiling. Specifically regarding rawhide drum skins, you'll want to treat it periodically with a hydrating oil, such as neatsfoot or mink oil, or some of the special formulae developed by drummers and drum retailers. Even shea butter will work, and is a nicely biodegradable option. The humidity in your area, what sort of weather your drum is exposed to, and even how much you play it (and where) can contribute to a dry hide.

Conversely, the other big threat is dampness. If a hide happens to get wet, either through rain or spillage, get it someplace where it can air-dry as soon as possible. Don't use a heat source, however, as this can excessively dry out the hide. Also, don't store the hide in a damp place.

Furs can pick up dust over time, along with other detritus, especially if the hair is long. I find it useful to shake the hides out every few weeks. Careful vacuuming (with a hose and attachment) can also be done about once a year as well. Dusty leather can be gently wiped with a damp cloth. Be careful with older hides to avoid tearing or otherwise damaging them.

Should a hide become dirty, clean it as soon as possible with a gentle soap and warm water, especially if it's been rolled in something that may be difficult to remove when dry. For a quick fix, most hides can be submerged in water for a brief time, just long enough to scrub them off, and then will need to be hung up to try immediately. Coats and other garments can be taken to a dry cleaner (bonus points if you have an environmentally friendly dry cleaner in your area); I've never tried taking a whole hide, ears, tail and all to the cleaners, though. You might ask your friendly neighborhood taxidermist for ideas on local resources. *Under no circumstances should you put any leather or fur in a clothes washer or dryer!* These machines will be too hard on them, and the dryer can dehydrate the skin. I know people who had hides fall to pieces with this treatment.

Fur that gets wet will end up with the hair in clumps when it dries. Simply rub the clumps of hair between your fingers, and the hairs should separate. If you wish, take a hair brush and gently brush the fur until it smoothes again. Also, don't leave fur in water longer than necessary; otherwise the hairs may start to slip, or fall out.

There may be situations where a simple bath won't help. If you end up with something sticky such as tree sap on a hide, you can use Goo Gone ™ or another similar gunk removal product. An accidental run-in with paint may be fixable with water, if it's acrylics, or a good soap if oil-based, though some may be permanent; the earlier you can get the paint off, the better the chance of avoiding staining. In the event something really smelly gets soaked in (such as a pet deciding to mark hir territory), you may need to give repeated baths mixed with airing out, and perhaps packing the hide in something nicer-smelling, such as cedar chips.

Unfortunately, there may be things that you can't remove. If it only affects a small part of the hide, you may be able to cut it off. However, more extensive dirt or damage may be permanent. Additionally, very old hides or hides that are in poor condition may not hold up to the rigors of a bath. In these cases, it may be best to retire the hides and give them a good place to sit, if the damage is such that they can't fulfill their previous purpose.

While we're on the subject of baths and water, avoid keeping your hides in a damp place. They can rot rather easily. If they get wet by accident, such as via rain or an accidental "bath", get them dried out as soon as possible. You can utilize a space heater if necessary — obviously, don't drape the hide directly over it! Instead, hang or drape it over a chair, and set up the space heater at least three feet away. Even if one side is dry, check the other.

One final thing I'd like to mention in regards to fur is

clothes moths. These little critters eat the hairs off of furs and leave nasty granular poo and other detritus behind on bare skin. They can do a lot of damage in a short time, so it's important to keep an eye out for them if you're in an area prone to them. If you see moths flitting near your furs, go check them. Whether there's damage or not, there are a few things you can do to prevent more problems.

First, take any affected hides, wrap them in a plastic bag, and stuff them in a freezer as cold as you can get it for at least two weeks. This will kill any eggs, larvae or hidden adult moths (you may want to make a conciliatory offering to the totem Clothes Moth in this case). If you have more furs than freezer space, rotate them through, and keep the post-freezer ones separate from the pre-freezer ones. Also, vacuum or otherwise clean the area where the skins were very well to get rid of any larvae and eggs left behind. Finally, you can sprinkle cedar chips liberally over the area where you'll keep the furs from here on out to discourage them, but also to avoid poisonous mothballs and other chemicals as much as possible. If you keep your hides in containers, consider a cedar chest, or airtight plastic bins.

Tanning Hides

I'll admit that I've never tanned a hide, fur or leather. Some of it has had to do with a distinct lack of space—apartments aren't particularly good places, especially where there are pets who may get into the chemicals and so forth. Additionally, I simply don't want to put in the amount of time it takes to properly clean, de-fat and cure a hide.

This, of course, has no bearing on your decision whether to try tanning for yourself (if you haven't already). In fact, I would imagine that this can allow you to gain an even stronger relationship with the spirits of the skins you tan. If you do want to give it a shot, you have a few options available to you:

--Rawhide isn't technically tanned; the hair is removed with a lime solution or other such agent, then dried.

--There are several commercial (chemical) tanning kits of varying qualities and prices available.

--Salt and alum tanning is relatively inexpensive and fairly common.

--Alcohol and turpentine tanning isn't as common, and is apparently better suited for smaller hair-on hides.

--Brain tanning is a "green" option, being chemical-free. It's also one of the oldest methods—and one of the most involved. You'll need to have a place where you can set up a fire to smoke the hide, and a lot of time to "work" the hide to make it soft. However, brain-tanned hides are quite popular, and the best ones exceptionally soft.

--Vegetable tanning utilizes bark as a tanning agent. It's generally used for leather, though very thin hair-on hides can be bark tanned if you're careful.

Here's a list of resources for further information:

http://www.braintan.com/barktan/1basics.htm (Bark Tanning)
http://www.state.tn.us/twra/pdfs/tanninghides.pdf (Salt and alum, alcohol and turpentine, and brain tanning)
http://www.nativetech.org/tanning/tanning.html (Detailed step-by-step description of brain tanning)
http://www.aaanativearts.com/article379.html (Making rawhide)
Deerskins Into Buckskins: How To Tan With Natural Materials, a Field Guide for Hunters and Gatherers by Matt Richards – a highly rated text on making deerskin leather

Perhaps some day I'll have the resources, time and patience to try it out for myself. In the meantime, let me know how it works for you!

Simple and Easy Leather Lacing

Leather lacing will come in handy on all sorts of projects. In addition to making good straps for tying, carrying, hanging, and wearing pouches, it's also used for wrapping metal hoops for wall hangings, necklaces for pendants, and straps for dance costumes, among others.

You can buy pre-cut leather lacing in a rainbow of colors, and from several types of hides. However, this can get expensive over time. Making leather lacing not only is cheaper, but it can also allow you to make use of scraps that may not be useful for other projects. There are machines that will take entire pieces of leather and cut them into side by side strips. However, again these cost money, and they don't work for smaller scraps that may not be long enough for one long lacing.

What I'd like to offer is a method that will work on all but the tiniest pieces of leather. You can cut as much lacing as you like from the piece, even if you just want a few inches to make a drawstring for a necklace pouch.

Next page: a piece of leather being cut into lacing by cutting around the outside edge. Center: piece of leather with narrow "peninsula" cut off. Right: starting your cut at an uneven spot. The little pointy tab to the right of the initial cut will still need to be trimmed from the final lace.

First, round off all the corners of the piece of leather. You don't need to make it a perfect circle or oval; just make sure that there aren't sharp corners, or "peninsulas" that are narrower than twice the length of the lacing you're cutting. Then, simply start cutting around the outer edge of the leather, making however wide a lacing you like. If there's a place along the edge where the leather is a bit uneven, this makes a good starting point. Cut in a continuing spiral around the leather until you either have enough lacing, or run out of leather. The smaller the piece of leather and the closer to the center you get, the less straight the lacing will be. It'll still work, and I personally like the "rustic" look of the slightly uneven edges, as compared to something that looks like it came out of a machine.

Top: Two lacing ends with slits in them. Center: Put one slitted end through the other, then lace the other end of the first through its own slit. Bottom: Pull tight to secure.

If you have a bunch of smaller lacings, you can easily connect them together without stitching or tying knots. If you haven't cut the lacings yet, when you do, make sure the last two inches at each end is a bit wider than the rest. Next, make a lengthwise slit at each end, leaving at least a quarter inch of uncut leather between the slit and the edge. Take two laces, and thread the end of one through the slit in the other. Then take the other end of the first lace, and run it through the slit at the other end. Pull tight, and repeat until you have a nice, long string of lacings bound together. I've made lacing this way out of scraps as small as 2" x 2".

You're going to want to reserve this for more durable hides, such as deerskin. Lacing made from thin hides has a tendency to break under stress, especially at places where the lacing curved around the hide. If you aren't sure whether a specific hide will work, cut a small piece of lacing, then tug hard at both ends.

A Few Miscellaneous Tips For Working With Hides

There are numerous styles of hand stitching. The two most simple are the running stitch and the whip stitch. A very simple running stitch is simply a line of in-and-out stitches. The whip stitch involves stitching while wrapping the thread around the outer edges of whatever you're stitching together. I prefer the whip stitch because it's neater and a little more forgiving if you want your stitches to be pretty. If I use a running stitch, I usually come back through a second time and stitch the opposite sides of the leather. Also, with larger projects, I'll usually double up my whip stitching as well.

However, this is all for hand stitching with glovers' needles and thinner thread. If you use an awl and thicker cord or a sewing machine, you shouldn't need double stitching for most projects.

If you're stitching two pieces of leather together, you can have the stitching on either the inside or outside of the final project on most projects. Make sure your stitches are even if you

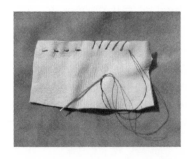 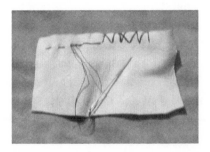

Left: Single simple running stitch (left) and simple whip stitch (right). Right: Doubled-up running and whip stitches.

have them on the outside so they look neater. With fur, you'll have to put the stitches on the inside unless the hairs are very thin or short. Place the two pieces of fur hair side together. Then tuck the stray hairs poking out of the edges in between the pieces. Don't worry about doing this for more than the two or so inches of the hide you'll be grasping at a time; just make sure the hairs are tucked in on the part you're about to stitch up each time you put the needle through.

Craft knives are especially useful for cutting fur. If you use scissors on fur, you'll also end up shearing off the ends of hairs around the edges. With a craft knife, you can easily slit the fur on the skin side without damaging the hair; with very thin hides, such as rabbit, cut most of the way through and then carefully pull the cut apart. You can also do more precision, detail cutting with a craft blade. However, I would suggest using scissors for longer cuts, such as cutting lacing out of a piece of leather.

If you're working with older fur or leather (though especially fur) that may tear when sewn, glue fabric to the back of it. Then you can stitch through the fabric and hide, and the stitches won't tear through the hide. This doesn't have to be anything really fancy; do make sure, though, that you stitch around all edges of the hide and fabric so you don't have ragged edges. For example, on a drawstring pouch (see the next chapter), the edge around the opening just needs a whip stitch all around it to neaten it up. If your fabric is really prone to fraying, apply a light coat of Mod Podge to it to keep the threads in place.

Another thing to keep in mind with old hides, as well as very thin ones, is that if you need to cut slits in it (such as for the drawstring pouch discussed in the next chapter), reinforce both ends of each slit to prevent the hide from further tearing, even if you back it with fabric. Simply throw a few whip stitches at the top and bottom of the slit. This is a preferred option to hole punches. If you aren't sure whether a hide will need a fabric backing, or reinforced slits, very carefully make a slit in it and gently pull it apart, gradually increasing the amount of force. If the fur begins to tear relatively quickly, err on the side of caution.

When working with any hide, you may find holes in inconvenient places. These are relatively easy to stitch up. With the back side facing you, fold the hole in half and bring the edges together. Then use a whip stitch to sew them tightly together. However, if it is a particularly large hole, you may want to patch it instead. Cut a piece of a similar hide that is a bit larger than the hole. Lay the front side of the patch over the back side of the hide. Then stitch it into place using a running stitch all around the edge.

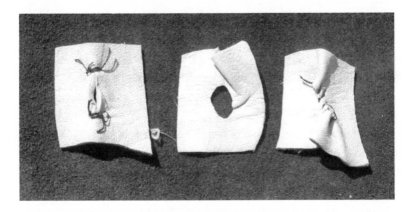

When painting leather, make sure that you've done as much other stuff to it (stitching, stretching on a frame, etc.) as possible beforehand. For example, if you want to stretch a piece of leather over a hoop, do the stretching and stitching before painting; otherwise your design may end up distorted. Or, if you want to paint a leather pouch, paint it after you've put the pouch together and turned it right side out. This will decrease the chance of crackling or other damage to the paint. However, if you're stitching beads or other items to a leather or fur pouch, do so before you put the pieces together — it makes it a lot easier when you can access both the front and back side of the hide!

You can do a small amount of painting on fur, mostly for accent purposes. Get a fan brush (a small paint brush whose bristles are spread out in a flat arc like a fan) and dry brush (without wetting the brush) small amounts of acrylic paint lightly onto the fur. I use this for accenting eyes on face skins a lot; most of the time otherwise I like to leave furs natural.

An assortment of leather and fur pouches.

Leather and Fur Pouches

What You'll Need:

-- A garment-weight leather, such as deerskin or lambskin, or fur
--Scissors or a sharp craft knife
--Needles/awl and thread
--Leather lacing (you can also substitute yarn, thick cord, etc.)
--Cutting board
--Optional: beads, paint and other decorations

Drawstring Pouches

1. Cut out two rectangles of hide the same size. For a necklace pouch (what's commonly known as a medicine pouch among pagans and New agers), the pieces should be about 3" wide by 4" long. A tarot/rune/etc. pouch should start with at least 6" wide by 8" tall, if not larger. Bigger pouches are quite possible, of course.

2. With your craft knife, cut four slits near the top of each piece of hide at equal intervals. Make sure there's at least ½" between the top of the slits and the edge of the hide, more for larger pouches. Reinforce them if necessary as described in the last chapter. Or, alternately, punch four holes in the leather with a hole punch or awl (make sure the holes are big enough for your lacing.

3. Put the two pieces of hide with the outsides (smoother side for leather, hair side for fur) together. Start stitching at one of the top corners. Put a few whip stitches at the very top to help strengthen the stress points where the pouch opens (as shown in the picture to the left). Then stitch all the way around the sides and bottom; when you get to the other upper corner, stabilize it with whip stitches as well. You may also choose to get back with a second set of stitches if you're using thinner thread or if the pouch is particularly large.

4. Alternately, if you're working with leather, you can stitch from the outside, if your edges are very evenly matched (with a running stitch or a stitching awl you can trim afterwards). Again, make sure you stabilize the upper corners near the opening of the pouch.

5. Once you're done stitching, turn the pouch inside out. Make sure you get the bottom corners turned out all the way. Be careful not to push too hard, though; you don't want to break the stitches.
6. Now it's time for lacing. If you've made a necklace pouch, you'll need a drawstring and a necklace string. The drawstring should be at least 6" long, preferably a bit longer. You want it long enough that it'll thread all the way around the pouch, and still have enough length left over to tie. Your necklace lacing should be at least 30" long, longer if you want the pouch to hang lower or if you are particularly tall. For a tarot-sized pouch, you'll need two drawstrings. Each one should be about four times as long as your pouch is wide.
7. For a necklace pouch, thread the lacing through all eight slits. Start at the front and put your drawstring into one of the two middle slits. Then bring it back out through the next slit closest to the stitching. Continue in and out all the way around the pouch. When you're done, you should have the two ends of the lacing sticking out of the two center slits in the front of the pouch. Directly behind the pouch should be a portion of the lacing that is on the outside of the back of the pouch between the two center slits in the back. Pull this part of the lacing out just a little bit to make a "hole". Now, take your necklace lacing and double it up. Take the loop in the middle and insert it up through the "hole" in the drawstring you just made, aiming towards the edge of the pouch. Then take the two ends of the necklace lacing and thread it through the loop. Pull the ends tight around the drawstring, then pull the drawstring tight as well. Your necklace pouch is now ready.

Left: Pull the loop of the necklace strap through the back of the drawstring. Center: Thread the ends of the necklace strap through the loop. Right: Pull the ends of the necklace strap tight around the drawstring and you're done!

8. For a tarot-sized pouch, take the end of one of your drawstrings and thread it into one of the slits nearest the stitching, then thread it out the next, and so forth. Continue all the way around the pouch until you have both ends of the drawstring sticking out at the same side of the pouch. Take your other drawstring, and where the first drawstring wraps around the side of the pouch opposite to where you had started stitching it, insert the second drawstring into one of the slits nearest to the stitching, and thread it through all the way around. You should now have drawstrings hanging out of each of the four slits closest to the stitching. Tie the ends of each pair of drawstrings together, and you're done!

Next page – First picture: A drawstring being threaded starting from the right side of the picture to the left. Second picture: The first drawstring has been threaded all the way around, and the second is started going from left to right. Third picture: You should have one set of drawstring ends at each side of the pouch. Pull them tight to close the pouch.

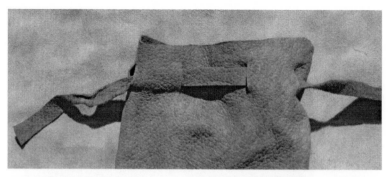

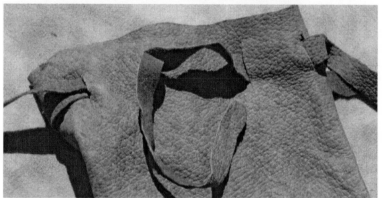

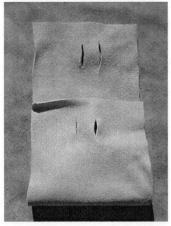

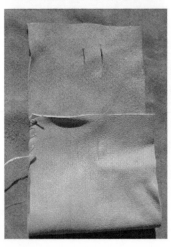

1. Get a piece of leather or fur that is slightly wider than you want your pouch to be, and three times longer. Fold the pouch over until it is roughly the size you'll want it to be when done. You'll want the flap to be even with or shorter than the bottom edge of the actual pouch portion. (See first picture on the left.)

the lower edge of the hide. Then lift the flap carefully, and make two slits on the front of the pouch portion as close as possible to where the slits in the flap will lie when the pouch is closed. (See second picture.)

3. If you're working with leather and want to stitch it from the outside, pick which edge you're going to start with first. Grasp the top corner of the front of the pouch portion and hold it tightly against the back of the pouch. (Just let the flap flop as it will.) Or, if you're going to stitch from the inside, very carefully mark with a pencil where the edge of the front of the pouch meets the back; make the mark on the inside of the hide, not the outside. Then fold the pouch inside out and carefully line up the top edge of the front of the pouch with the mark you made. (Third

picture shows where to start stitching, whether from the inside or outside.)

4. Insert a few whip stitches at this top corner as you did with the drawstring pouches above to strengthen the opening of the pouch. Stitch all the way down the edge, and back up if you want to double-stitch. Repeat on the other side, making sure that you line up the edges of the hides so your pouch doesn't end up lopsided.

5. Once you're done with the stitching, turn the pouch right side out again. You may find the flap to be a little too large now; trim it as you see fit.

6. Cut enough lacing to make a strap; if you just want the pouch to hang on a wall, you won't need much. If you want this to be a shoulder bag, cut a long portion and drape it over your shoulder to see how long you need it to be. Also, cut a 6" long piece of lacing for holding the flap closed.

7. To attach the shoulder/etc. strap, hold the pouch at either end of the top fold of the flap, just above where the stitching ends —

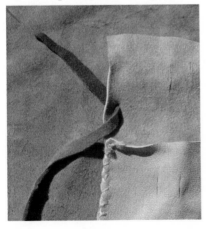

like a purse strap. Play around with it a bit to find how it hangs the best. When you have it where you want it, note exactly where you're holding it. Make slits that run parallel to the edges of the pouch at least ½" away from the edges, and make them just a little longer than your strap is wide. Thread one end of the strap through one of these slits and double it back on itself. Then stitch the strap to itself; you'll want to use a lot of stitches since these will be bearing all the weight of the pouch and its contents. Repeat on the other side, making sure the strap isn't twisted before you start stitching.

Alternately, you can tie the strap in a knot if it's thin enough and you don't mind the knots.

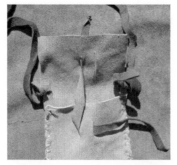

8. Open up the flap. Thread the six inch piece of lacing into one of the slits on the front of the pouch, and out of the other, so the ends dangle down the front of the pouch. Fold the flap over, and thread the lacing through the slits on it. Then tie the lacing together, which will hold the flap closed.

This is the easiest variation of the foldover pouch. You can make the pouch portion out of one double-over piece of hide, and then attach a separate flap, or you can make the entire pouch and flap out of three different pieces of hide. You can even mix and match various sorts of leather and fur to your heart's content! I like to take very small scraps of leather and fur and make little-bitty foldover pouches that are only two inches square, if that.

Chokers and Bracelets

The directions are essentially the same for both chokers and bracelets; size is the only difference. You'll want to use a softer, garment-weight leather such as deerskin, or a fur that isn't scratchy.

1. Cut out a strip of hide to the desired size. For a choker, take your neck measurement and subtract 2"; for a bracelet, your wrist measurement minus one inch. Make the hide however wide you

want, though for strips more than two inches wide you may want to round off the corners.

2. Make a slit across each end of the strip, leaving at least ¼ inch between the end of the slit and the edge of the hide; reinforce if necessary.

3. Cut two pieces of lacing of an equal length, with one end of each a little wider than the rest of the lacing. For chokers, lacings should be at least eight inches long, and at least six inches for bracelets.

4. Cut a vertical slit in the wider end of each lacing, with at least ¼" between the end of the slit and the edge of the lacing. Then take the slit end of one lacing and thread it through the slit on one end of the choker/bracelet. Thread the end of the lacing through the slit on the lacing, and pull tight so that the lacing is now looped around the end of the choker/bracelet. Repeat with the other lacing. You're now done, other than whatever decorations you may want to add.

Left: Insert the lacing through the slit in the end of the choker/bracelet, then put one end of the lacing through the slitted end of the other, and pull tight. Right: a completed undecorated choker.

Wall Hangings

What You'll Need:

--A sturdy hoop; metal ones are readily available at craft stores, or even by disassembling the metal frames of lamp shades. You may also make a hoop out of willow branches or other pliable wood.
--Leather lacing
--Glue
--A piece of leather or fur big enough to stretch all the way across the hoop in at least some places; it doesn't have to cover the entire hoop, but it should have at least three "anchor points", places where the leather will double over the hoop back onto itself.
--Artificial sinew or a similar weight of cord
--Scissors or craft knife
--Needles/awl and thread, or leather lacing that is at least six inches longer than the circumference of the hoop
--A small clamp, or two heavy books/other flat objects

Wrapping the Hoop

This will be the basis for the next two projects.

1. Cut enough leather lacing to be able to wrap around the hoop; this may vary depending on the thickness of the hoop. For a standard thin metal hoop, I find that cutting lacing that is three times as long as the circumference of the hoop will be ample, and give you plenty left over for making a loop to hang it with.
2. Put a small spot of glue on the underside of one end of the lacing. Start wrapping the leather around the hoop; the first time around, wrap the leather around itself to help hold the glued portion in place, then continue wrapping, keeping the edges of the lace touching as you do so that the metal doesn't show. You may need to hold the glued part in place for the first few wraps to keep it from being pulled out of place.

3. When you reach the end of the lacing, or when you make it all the way back to where you started off, put glue on the end of the lacing, and make sure to wrap it tightly. Then clamp that portion of the hoop to keep the lacing in place, or put it between two books and let it dry.

4. If your lacing wasn't long enough, cut another one, and again put glue on the end. Make your first few wraps over the end of the last piece of lacing and the beginning end of the new piece, then continue wrapping.

5. If you have extra lacing once you get all the way around, put glue on the underside of the part of the lacing that will be the last bit wrapped around the hoop. After wrapping it, take the remaining lacing and tie it in a knot around the hoop. Tie another knot just in the leather right up against the first knot you made. Let the glue dry. If there's a long enough piece of lacing, you can double it up and tie an overhand knot in it to make the hanging loop. Otherwise just use another piece of lacing to make a hanging loop.

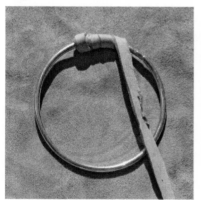 

Left: Starting to wrap the hoop. The end of the lacing has been glued in place, and then the rest of the lacing has been wrapped over it a few times before continuing to wrap clockwise. Right: The hoop is wrapped, and a knot has been tied in the end of the lacing to hold it in place.

Leather Wall Hanging

Popularly called a "medicine shield" or, especially among New Agers, "mandala", the basic structure of this wall hanging is a hoop (usually metal these days) with a piece of hide stretched over it or otherwise suspended from it. They're commonly used by neopagans and their ilk as leather canvasses for painting symbols and depictions of deities, spirits, or sacred events, or to serve as a personal standard.

1. Take your wrapped hoop and stretch the piece of leather or fur over it. It may cover the entire hoop, or only portions of it. If the hide covers the entire hoop, you may opt to not wrap the hoop at all, since no one will be able to see it anyway.
2. If the hide covers the entire hoop, you'll want to stitch it to the hoop all the way around. Make sure the hoop is as close to the center of the hide as possible. Fold the hide over the hoop so that the edge of the hide meets the back of the hide, like this:.

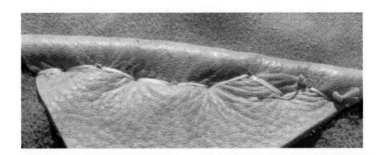

3. If you are using a needle and thread, simply stitch your way all the way around with a running stitch, and make sure you have a big, fat knot at the end of your thread to keep it from pulling through the hide. Try to stitch as close to the hoop as possible. (See picture above for a sample of a slightly sloppy, but serviceable running stitch to this effect.)

4. If you are using leather lacing to attach the hide to the hoop, you'll need to cut or punch holes for it first; if cutting, make the slits horizontal, or parallel to the hoop. Carefully hold the folded-over hide in place as you make the cuts/holes in both layers. Then weave the lacing through the holes/slits either run a running stitch or whip stitch, leaving a few inches of lacing at the beginning. Once you've made it all the way around, tie the two ends of the lacing together.

5. If the hide only covers parts of the hoop in multiple places, you'll need to attach each "anchor point" separately. I find needle and thread stitching to be easier, but you can also use the leather lacing option as well. Make sure that as you attach each anchor point, you pull the hide as tight as you can.

6. If you don't already have a hanging loop left over from wrapping the hoop in leather, simply take a piece of lacing and either loop it around the hoop if there's an opening, or make a very small slit in the hide at the top of your wall hanging if the hoop is completely covered, and thread the lacing through that. Hold the end together and tie them in an overhand knot.

Left: A leather wall hanging with "anchor points", rather than a skin that entirely covers the hoop. Also note the hanging loop made from the long end of the lacing left over from wrapping the hoop. Right: A rawhide wall hanging. Notice how the lacing wraps around the hoop and through the holes in the hide. The ends of the lacing are tied together around the hoop at the top.

Rawhide Wall Hanging

For this wall hanging you'll specifically want a piece of rawhide. Even rawhide from dog chew toys will work.[65]

1. Soak the rawhide in water until it's soft and pliable. Thicker rawhide may take a while.

2. While still wet, stretch the rawhide out as flat as you can get it.

---

[65] Just as a barely related side note, those rawhide chews aren't that great for dogs anyway. In addition to the chemicals that are used in bleaching the hide, the rawhide itself can be deadly. An overly exuberant chewer can gnaw off a sizable chunk of rawhide and swallow it. If it absorbs enough stomach juices and swells up, it can cause an obstruction in the digestive system and cause a quick but agonizing death — if not removed by expensive emergency surgery! Keep the regular rawhide bones for your art projects, and give your dog boiled beef knuckle bones, or chew toys made of ground-up and pressed rawhide.

Cut a circle out of it just a little smaller than the inside circumference of your wrapped hoop.

3. Punch a series of holes around the outside of the rawhide circle, leaving at least ½" of leather between the holes and the edge of the hide. Or, use scissors to cut holes in the hide — I find it easiest to double the hide over and cut a triangle in both layers of the hide, which will result in diamond-shaped holes. (Remember when you were a kid and you folded over a piece of paper, then cut half a heart shape in it which then unfolded to make a whole heart shape? It's the same concept here.)

4. Lay the rawhide between two big books or other flat, heavy objects, and let it dry thoroughly. (You can also layer towels in there if you're worried about the books getting wet.

5. Once it's dry, put it in the center of the hoop. Tie a piece of sinew/cord to the hoop, then thread the end of the sinew through the nearest hole in the rawhide. Wrap the sinew over the hoop, and then back through the next hole in the rawhide. Repeat until you've threaded all the holes in the rawhide.

6. Tie the end of the sinew around the hoop securely.

Decorate your wall hanging however you like; acrylic paints work especially well on both leather and rawhide.

Dance Costumes

Many pagans enjoy drum circles and other opportunities to dance. You can create dance costumes to not only honor the skin spirits, but also totems and other beings. These should not, however, be used as simple Halloween costumes; they are sacred ritual tools that house spirits within them.

What You'll Need:

--Animal hides (specifics will be given further below)
--Leather lacing

--Scissors or craft knife
--Needles and thread
--Newspaper and sinew/cord
--Sharpie or similar marker
-- Glue, leather scraps

Mask/Headdress

For this you'll need the mask (face skin) of a mammal. Coyotes and foxes are good choices, though I've made masks and headdresses from the skins of wolves, beavers, bobcats, and other medium to large mammals. Some of the businesses in Appendix A have a selection of mask skins. I would strongly suggest buying a mask skin that's already been removed from the rest of the hide, rather than buying a whole hide and cutting off the head.

1. Many mask skins, especially those with prominent ears such as coyotes or foxes, will end up somewhat squished somewhere between skinning and shipment. The ears may be crumpled down, the muzzle might be folded over, and so forth. First, soak the mask skin in water until the ears and muzzle are soft. Be aware that the nose and lips, as well as the very end of the muzzle, may be very tough. It's important not to leave the fur in water too long, so that the hairs don't start falling out. Fifteen to thirty minutes is usually a good window of time. If you have to work at the ears and muzzle a bit, it's okay—you just want them to be soaked enough to be somewhat softer than before.

2. To perk the ears up again, create cones out of balled up paper, and set them into the inside of the ears, molding the ears around them. Then take a length of sinew and wrap it around the ears several times to hold the paper in. (If you've ever splinted ears on dogs with "up" ears, such as German Shepherd dogs, it's the same concept.)

3. For the muzzle, stretch it out as much as you can, then stuff it

with paper as you did the ears, and wrap with sinew. You can also stuff the rest of the head as well. Be careful not to pull the sinew too tight, or you'll end up with creases in the hide. Make it just tight enough to hold the paper in place. This may take some practice, and you may have to get creative to get things just right, but over time it gets easier.

4. Let the mask skin dry completely before removing the paper and sinew. This may take a few days. You can speed the process up with a space heater, but make very sure you keep it far enough away from the skin to not start a fire! If it's the middle of summer and blazing hot, the heat will do the work for you.

5. If you need to reshape part of the mask, just submerge that part in water, being careful not to get the parts that are finished wet. You may also find it helpful to stitch parts of the mask to reshape them; for example, if an ear is lopsided, it may help to tack down one side of it with a few good stitches to get it upright again. Also, if there are holes in the skin, stitching them closed may make the mask look better.

6. Once you have the mask skin the way you want it, it's time to add straps. Place the mask either over your face if it is large enough, or over the top of your head. Pull the mask tight over your face/head; notice where the best places to hold it are.

7. Make slits on your marks. If you use slits, reinforce both ends of each slit with a few stitches.

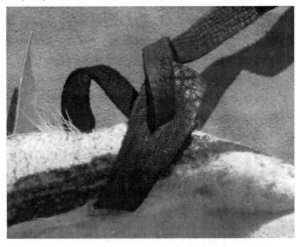

Above: A lacing threaded through the slit in the mask where you made your mark. The non-slitted end of the lacing has been threaded though the slitted end, and then will be pulled tight. (See steps 6-9)

8. Cut two equal length pieces of leather lacing, with the last two inches of one end of each a little wider than the rest. Cut the lace long enough so that if you place one end of it at the very top of your head and let it drape down the side of your head, the other end is at least six inches past your chin. Make a vertical slit in the wider ends of the lacings.

9. Thread one end of one lacing through one of the slits in the mask skin. Then thread the non-slitted end of the lacing through the slit in the other end of the lacing, and pull tight. Repeat with other lacing and other side of the mask.

10. If you are creating a true mask (again, this works better with larger animals such as wolves or larger coyotes, not foxes), you'll probably need to make the eye holes bigger. Place the mask over your face and see where the skin is blocking your view the most. Then carefully cut away the skin around the eyes with the craft knife, keeping the shape roughly oval/almond-shaped. Keep trying the mask on, and check a mirror, too, to see how it looks.

Tail

This project can be done with just about any mammalian tail, from bobcat to wolf. One of the exceptions is horse tails, which are too thick to stitch. I'll have instructions for horse tails later in the chapter. You can make a tail to match your mask, or just by itself.

1. Your tail should be in good shape; if the hide seems dry or tears easily, find the skin side of the base of the tail where it would connect to the rest of the body. With thicker fur, this may be a bit of a task! Once you have found that part of the skin, glue a small scrap of leather to it. This will help to stabilize it once you start stitching. Once the glue is dry, you can proceed with the project.

2. If your tail happens to be twisted or bent (this especially happens with thin tails, such as the tail of the ringtail), you can soak it in water as per the directions earlier in the chapter. Then lay it flat between two heavy books. Or, if it is a thick fluffy tail like fox, carefully tie a cord to each end of the tail, gently pull the tail straight, and either tie the cord to stationary objects (such as table legs) or pin them between two heavy books. Let the tail dry thoroughly before proceeding.

3. Cut a long piece of leather lacing; you'll want it to be the size of your waistline, plus at least eighteen inches. Make sure it's at least ½ inch wide as well. If necessary connect multiple lacings together with the method discussed earlier in this chapter.

4. Fold the lacing in half so you know where the center is. Then find the center of the skin side of the tail at the base. Align the two centers, with the smooth side of the leather facing the skin side of the tail.

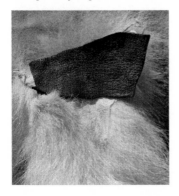 

Left: A piece of leather about to be trimmed and glued to the base of the skin side of a tail to give it more strength. Right: Lacing stitched into place. In this picture the tail actually has two separate laces stitched to it, but the concept is the same.

5. Stitch the leather and the tail together using a running stitch. You'll want to stitch across the tail at least three times. You may have a little trouble pulling the thread through if the hairs get caught up in the thread; just do your best to pull them out, then pull the stitch tight.

Horse Tail

This also works for smaller tails that still have the bones in them and therefore can't be stitched. Obviously for smaller tails you'll need less leather, but the point is the same.

1. If your horse tail is dirty, give it a quick bath in warm water and mild soap or shampoo and let it dry.
2. Find a scrap of leather that will wrap over the base of the horse tail, covering as much of the top three inches as possible. Use a piece of sinew (and glue, if you like) to hold the leather in place; trim the ends of the sinew as short as you can.

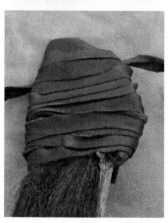

3. Cut a length of leather lacing that is the equivalent of your waistline, plus six feet. If necessary, connect multiple pieces of lacing as described earlier in the chapter. Make sure it's at least ½ inch wide.

4. Find the center of the lacing. Center it on the leather you wrapped around the base of the tail, near the bottom edge of the leather, on the top side of the horse tail. (See top left picture.)

5. Now wrap the lacing *tightly* in both directions around the leather, and cross them as they meet on the bottom (skin) side of the horse tail. (See bottom left picture.)

6. Continue to wrap in this fashion, crossing the lacings each time they meet, and wrapping higher up the tail each time. Make sure the edges of the lacing meet with each pass around the tail. If you like, spot-glue the underside of the lacing as you wrap.

7. Once you are an inch away from the end of the horse tail, tie the two laces tightly together in a square knot on the bottom side of the tail. Your tail is ready to wear!

107

Full Skin

These are instructions for making a dance costume out of a whole mammal skin, which includes the main pelt of the body, the head, all four legs, and the tail. The legs do not necessarily have to have the feet and claws, and the head may be missing some or all of the face, though it should at least have the ears. While this pattern can be used with just about any full skin, it's optimized for larger skins such as coyote or wolf. For smaller skins, you may find the points at which you bind the skin to your body may be different.

1. Make any necessary repairs, ear/muzzle fixes, and cleaning of the skin. If the skin has been barrel or case skinned, meaning that the belly hasn't been split open, then you'll need to open it. You can do this by turning the skin inside-out by pulling the front end through the back end, then taking a craft blade and carefully cutting down the center of the belly side of the skin. You may have to use scissors when you get to the lower jaw skin, which can be pretty tough.

2. Drape the head of the pelt over your head, and note where the best place to hold it to your head. Mark these places and add leather lacings as you would with the mask/headdress above.

3. With the pelt tied to your head, note where the forelegs are in relation to your body. Depending on the size of the skin and of your own body, they will most likely either be at your neck or your arms.

4. If the forelegs are near your neck, you'll want to wrap them around your neck/shoulders like a cape. Add lacings to the ends of the forelegs. The easiest way to do this is to make two parallel vertical slits near the ends of the forelegs. Reinforce them with stitches at each end. Then take a single leather lacing at least six inches long, with a slit at one end, and thread it in one slit and out the other. Thread the non-slitted end of the lacing through the slit at the other end, and pull tight. Repeat with the other lacing and

foreleg. You'll now be able to tie these together.

5. If the forelegs will lie along your arms, make slits in the end of the forelegs.

6. Add leather lacings to these slits. You can then tie these together around your arms or wrists. (See picture below.)

7. If the end of the foreleg meets your hand, make two vertical slits in the end of the foreleg as in step 4. Take a leather lacing that is at least eighteen inches long; it does not need a slit at one end. Put each end 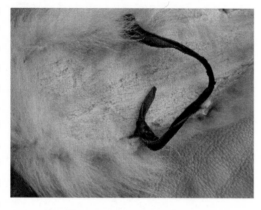 into one of the vertical slits, starting on the fur side of the skin, so the ends end up on the skin side.

8. Now, drape the end of the skin over your hand. Take the loop created by the leather lacing, and put your middle finger through it. Pull the lacing out as much as you need for the skin to lie comfortably along your arm when your arm is completely extended. Tie the ends of the lacings in a knot so that the loop stays that size. (See next page for pictures.)

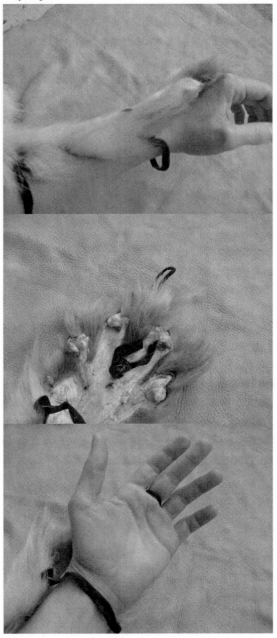

9. With the skin tied to your head, stand up. See where the ends of the back legs are. If they are at your waist line, then add lacings to them as you would in step 3. Make sure you give yourself at least six extra inches per lacing for tying.

10. If the ends of the back legs meet your legs, make two vertical slits in the end of each as in step 4. Next, cut two lacings that are at least twelve inches longer than the measurement around the part of your leg where you'll be tying the skin. You do not need slits at the ends of the lacings.

11. Starting on the fur side, thread one lacing into one of the slits, and out the other. Pull the lacing through until there's an equal amount of lacing on each side of the leg skin. Repeat with the other lacing and leg (see picture below).

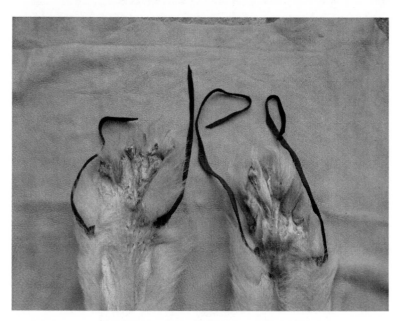

12. Now, try the costume on and see how it fits all together. Make any necessary adjustments.

Variations may include:

--A headless pelt worn in a cape style
--A very small pelt, such as skunk or rabbit, worn as a headdress, or as part of a belt
--Leg skins tied to the arms/legs, maybe with a mask/headdress and/or tail added.

One Final Note (or Beat?)

I was originally going to include completed instructions on how to make a rawhide frame drum. However, I've only ever made one myself, and when I went to explain how I did it, I ended up essentially giving the same information that I found in the instructions that came in the kit that I used. So to avoid repetition, I highly recommend the frame drum kits available at Cedar Mountain Drums (http://www.cedarmtn  drums.com/). The one I made on my very first attempt (the smaller one in the picture) ended up with a lovely sound, and was my journeying drum[66] when I first started practicing shamanism in earnest

---

66 That is until a fox squirrel that was living in the unfinished attic of our first apartment in Portland accidentally got into the finished portion that was our shared ritual room. In the ensuing chaos of trying to catch a half-crazed Oregonian squirrel with a milk crate and a peacock feather, a cup of paint water ended up spilled on the

Chapter Six: Bones, Skulls, and Other Hard Stuff

The Skinny on Bones

Bones are largely comprised of a hard mineral casing and soft marrow center (except in birds, whose bones are hollow, and cartilaginous fish). The skeleton is the main supporting structure of a vertebrate animal, giving shape to the creature as well as helping to protect vital organs, especially in the chest cavity. The skull, of course, houses the brain, as well as the eyes and some respiratory passages. And they support the muscles for activities like motion. Bones are even instrumental in hearing, with the "hammer, anvil and stirrup" being key players.

The insides of bones are equally important. They produce hematopoietic blood cells; these are immature cells which can be converted into any of the full-fledged blood cells, such as those for carrying oxygen, or boosting immune functions. Bones also may store fats and minerals for the rest of the body's use, as well as collecting toxins from the rest of the body and removing them through careful excretion.

Most bones are well-concealed (unless something goes wrong, like an injury). Teeth are a notable exception. Antlers in deer are also made of bone, and during the time the antlers are in velvet they're living, growing tissue.[67] Similarly, the ribbed newt and the Anderson's salamander can shove their ribs through poisonous glands, and then further out through their skins, which essentially lines them with venom-tipped daggers. (Isn't nature *awesome?*)

---

[67] Anonymous, 2009

Horns, on the other hand, are made of keratin (except for the horns of rhinos, which are actually compressed hair). They are not shed, except for rare instances such as the pronghorn antelope, which still has a bone core for new horns to form around. Claws and bird beaks are bone with a wrapper of keratin, similar to our fingernails.

Many mammals will chew on bones for the calcium content. Some of the prettiest antlers I have are ones that have patterns of rodents' tooth marks etched into them.

Where to Get Bones (and Antlers, and Horns....)

Because bones are more durable, these are the easiest finds if you prefer to be a scavenger in the woods, fields and roadsides. If you have legal access to private land, so much the better; public lands, especially those with a lot of visitors, will often be picked over in short time.

Should you be in an area where you can legally pick up roadkill, please, please be careful. Do so during the day when possible. Park your vehicle well off the road, some distance from the roadkill so you won't be hidden by it, and approach the roadkill as far away from traffic as possible.

When scavenging bones, wear disposable rubber gloves to pick them up, and stick it in a plastic bag. Toss it in the trunk if you have one, or the bed, or otherwise as far away as possible (if it's still stinky, you'll be particularly motivated to do this). Do be aware that certain diseases can be contagious through remains — this includes everybody's favorite, rabies! (The saliva and brains, for example, still have the virus in them after a recent death — no bite required.) When in doubt, just leave the carcass to rot where it is, and scavenge the bones once they're well cleaned by Nature.

If you have a friendly neighborhood taxidermist, check with hir to see if s/he has any spare bones that s/he doesn't need. Additionally, butchers often have bones available that will just end up tossed out anyway. Or, if you're an omnivore, cut out the bone of a cut of meat prior to cooking (cooking can weaken bones, especially smaller ones).

Of course, if you don't want to put in all that effort, you can procure bones through reputable online retailers. I've mentioned a few in appendix A. Do be aware that if you are outside of the United States, you may have some limits to what you can purchase and from whom. Most sites will place the responsibility for knowing legalities on the customer.

Another option for those who aren't particular about what sort of bone they're working with is bone beads. Generally speaking they'll be made from cow, sheep or camel bones, though they may not always be labeled. You can either get these from dealers in beads and/or animal remains, or by hitting up thrift stores for jewelry. Be aware of how to tell bone from plastic; the latter will almost invariably be perfectly smooth other than seams on the side from the molding process, and in most cases is just a touch more lightweight. Additionally, the inside (and occasionally outside) of bone beads may sometimes show small holes that are naturally a part of the bone. If all else fails, buy some bone beads and compare them to plastic ones to get an idea of the differences. Sound is a particularly useful criterion; I've learned to distinguish bone from plastic by the way my fingernail sounds tapping against a bead.

There are also beads made out of bison or water buffalo horn; they usually come in black, or a deep, rich red, though a lovely amber is also available. They are usually polished to a glossy finish, and are quite smooth. They aren't as common as bone beads, especially in thrift store jewelry, but are readily available online.

Flea markets occasionally are a good place to find antlers. This includes not only small mounts with the antlers and skullcap, but even full-sized taxidermy mounts.

Why You Want to Clean Bones Thoroughly

There are a number of diseases that can be passed on through decaying flesh and marrow (the latter of which can stay intact in a bone for years). Among these are tetanus, rabies, distemper, and blood poisoning, among others. If you're really concerned about safety, limit yourself to professionally cleaned bones from reliable sources. To reduce the chances of disease transmission, handle uncleaned bones with rubber or cloth gloves. Make sure you wash your collecting clothing thoroughly, and if you used cloth gloves, soak them in diluted bleach. Wash your hands well; Searfoss recommends a 10% bleach solution. When you bring the bones home, let them sit overnight in a diluted bleach solution, then wash them with soap and warm water and let them air dry.[68]

Cleaning Bones

If you have bones (not horns!) that need cleaning, you can toss them in a pot of boiling water (make sure it's a pot you won't need for cooking again) until the flesh starts to fall off. Drill holes in the larger bones, such as pelvic bones and large leg bones, to help clean out the marrow inside.[69] The night before, soak them in water with a small amount of ammonia. The next day, you can boil them in that same water. A word of advice: if you can do this outdoors, so much the better, because this can get really smelly! Use tongs to pull the bones out to check on them, or prior to boiling tie some string to them that can be used to lift them.

A few tips are in order when boiling skulls. Too much boiling can cause the pieces of the skull to fall apart as they are held together by small bits of flesh. Additionally, teeth can fall out. Be sure you have some glue available after everything's clean

---

[68] Searfoss, 1995
[69] If you don't want to holes to show, once the bones are clean mix some white glue with either bone dust or flour and use it as a filler.

and dry if this happens. Additionally, teeth are prone to splitting if they're cooled too quickly, so don't put the skulls directly into colds water right after boiling; if it's cold outside, you may want to stick them in some hot (not boiling) water and let everything cool to help them adjust.[70]

Boiling works best for larger bones; smaller or more fragile ones can be submerged in a container of hydrogen peroxide overnight. Make sure you have a tight lid on the container. You may still need to manually clean off some flesh, but it will be easier as the peroxide will soften it significantly. The peroxide method also works if you have a bone that just has a bit of flesh on one end; submerge the end of the bone, then use plastic wrap to seal the opening of the container.[71]

Another option is maceration; this simply means letting the bones sit in a solution such as bleach and water for a period of days or weeks. Obviously it's slower and involves more decay than boiling, but it may be a better option for some people. 1.5% ammonia or bleach (in water) is the recommended ratio. Use a soft cloth and an old toothbrush to help clean off the decaying flesh. (Just a note: if you don't have a lot of room between you and your neighbors, you may want to avoid this method.)

You will definitely want to make sure all the flesh is removed, as well as the greasy residue on the surface of the bone. I've occasionally used sandpaper or the sanding bit of a Dremel to get rid of very stubborn bits of flesh. If you're working with a skull, make sure to clean the brains out, and to get all the little nooks and crannies. For degreasing, let them sit in a pot of 10% bleach or ammonia and 90% hot water for an hour. Then make another bucket or pot of the same components, and dip each bone in individually, then wipe with a soft cloth. Dry in a well-

---

[70] Searfoss, 1995
[71] Various, 2005

ventilated room or outside, for several days.[72]

Another method of degreasing involves letting the bones sit in a solution of water and Dawn dish soap. Interestingly, those who suggest it recommend that the water be heated, either on a really hot day, or by putting an aquarium heater in the water. It's also recommended for ammonia baths as well.[73]

Some people who work with a lot of bones on a regular basis will buy a package of dermestid beetles and put them in a terrarium with the bones. In a few weeks these little critters can strip the flesh, leaving nice clean bones.[74] I've heard anecdotally that mealworms (the kind that are sold as reptile food in pet stores) also will work, though I've not tried it. The same goes for putting the bones on an anthill. I would not recommend burying bones that have a significant amount of flesh on them unless you have some sort of wire cage to bury them in. Roving animals may dig up the bones to get at the meat. Additionally, the cage helps to keep the bones together so you're not digging a huge hole to try to find all of them.

For disinfection and whitening, hydrogen peroxide works well. I've tried diluted bleach; however, this can actually damage the bone if it's not diluted enough or if the bones are left in too long. The outer layer of bone will start to flake off after time. Glenn Searfoss, in his excellent text *Skulls and Bones*, recommends a 1.5% ammonia/98.5% water solution, or a similar ratio of bleach to water; his work was instrumental in the formation of this section.[75] I will say from personal experience that using too much bleach, while it may be tempting to the impatient (ahem), will leave your bones white but flaky, and more fragile. You can also

---

[72] Searfoss, 1995

[73] Various, 2009

[74] If you want to get a relatively inexpensive starter set of dermestid beetles, as well as informative DVDs and other info, check out http://www.dermestidbeetlecolonies.com/.

[75] Searfoss, 1995

try leaving the bones in the sun for a couple of weeks, though again damage can happen from weathering.

For more information here are a few websites:

http://community.livejournal.com/furhideandbone (good place to ask questions)
http://www.skullsite.com/misc/macerationmanual.htm (includes some detailed directions specifically for bird bones and skulls)
http://www.wc.adfg.state.ak.us/index.cfm?adfg=wildlife_news.view_article&articles_id=27&issue_id=11

A Note on Claws and Beaks

Because claws are covered in keratin, and beaks are simply part of the skull covered in skin, they need to be handled differently if you want them to stay intact. The leather on the beak will come off like any other flesh, so if you're submerging a bird skull in hydrogen peroxide to clean it, make sure the beak stays above the peroxide (this may take some creative suspension with string and found objects!). With claws, your best bet may simply be to clean off any remaining flesh with a sharp knife or a Dremel.

Physical Care of Bones

Bones really don't need too much in the way of care once they're cleaned. If left outside they will decay over time, and small animals may gnaw on them. Moisture will also promote decay over time, and can also cause growth of moss and other minute plants. However, if you like the weathered look, leaving the bones out in the elements for a few seasons can age them nicely.

You may wish to seal the bones for long-term protection. Transparent wax (such as paraffin), varnish, polyurethane, acrylic spray, or floral spray all will work. These will, of course, affect the texture and look of the bones, but will help preserve them longer.

Some finishes, such as wax, may attract dust, and polyurethane discolors if exposed to sunlight too long.[76]

Scapula Wall Hanging

I love shoulder blades. They've such a neat shape, and they make for a wonderful canvas. They're also excellent for novice carvers who want to do simple line carvings — though if you aren't careful you can end up going right through the thinnest parts of the bone on smaller scapulae (cow scapulae are a good starting point).

What You'll Need:

--One scapula (I'm partial to deer, but any will work)
--Pencil
--Acrylic paints, paintbrushes, and acrylic sealer spray, and/or Dremel with carving and drill bits
--Leather lacing
--(Optional) Waxed cord or artificial sinew, beads, feathers

1. Lightly sketch the design you want on the flat side of the scapula, with the narrow end up.
2. Carve and/or paint the design on the bone. If you'll be doing both, carve first, then paint. If you painted, seal the paint with acrylic sealer spray.
3. If you like, take the Dremel and drill a few holes along the bottom edge of the scapula. Then use these to tie "dangles" to your wall hanging — you can make them with feathers, beads, or whatever dangly things you'd like to add.
4. Take a piece of leather lacing at least twelve inches long. Wrap it around the "neck" of the scapula, and tie a square knot in the back, then tie the two ends together with an overhand knot. It's now ready to hang!

---

[76] Searfoss, 1995

Deer Antler Wall Hanging

If you have a single antler, all those tines and curves are wonderful for decoration!

What You'll Need

--A whitetail or mule deer antler
--Artificial sinew
--Dremel
--Beads and other adornment; acrylic paint and sealer

1. To hang items on the ends of tines, you'll want to drill holes in the ends; otherwise your sinew will slip off.
2. If desired, paint the antler. Let the paint dry, then seal it.
3. String beads and other items on lengths of artificial sinew with a knot at one end to keep them from slipping off. Tie the other end through the holes at the ends of the tines or around the beams

in between the tines.

4. Tie a piece of sinew around the base of the antler; make sure there are long ends of sinew left. Then tie the tips of those ends together to make a loop—now you have something to hang the antler from!

Skull Rattle

Depending on how large a brain casing a skull has, you'll get various volumes and pitches of rattle. Whitetail deer tend to have quieter, higher pitched rattles; black bears are deeper and louder. What you put in the brain casing also affects the sound; heavier items, such as buckshot or pebbles, will make a louder noise than beans or seeds. Do be aware that heavier things can wear away the bone quicker over time.

What You'll Need:

--A skull (larger mammals work best; avoid skulls with larger antlers)
--A deer tibia (lower leg bone) with one end cut off, or a dowel rod; no matter what you use, make sure it fits snugly into the hole at the base of the skull
--Buckshot, pebbles, small glass or bone beads, beans, seeds
--JB Weld
--Air-drying clay (I use Crayola's Model Magic ™ clay)
--(Optional) Acrylic paints, paintbrushes, acrylic paint sealer, leather lacing, fur scraps

1. Put a small handful of pebbles/beans/etc. into the brain casing. Hold your hand over the hole, and shake the skull to see how it

123

sounds. Add or remove items until you have the sound you want. If you have things popping out of the sinus cavities, either use larger items, or use a different skull. You may also stick some air-drying clay into the sinus passages; make sure it dries thoroughly before you continue.

2. Insert the tibia/dowel rod into the hole at the base of the skull. Mix up a generous amount of JB Weld and fill as much of the gaps between the skull and handle as possible; if there is a significant gap, just try to get as much JB Weld into the crevices between the skull and handle as possible. If the hole is larger than the handle to the point where you can hold the handle in the center of the hole and there's absolutely no contact between the two, get a smaller skull or larger handle. Set aside to dry with the skull laid on its side, as close to horizontal as possible. If necessary, prop the handle in place with objects underneath it, and put other objects on either side of the skull to keep it from tipping.

3. Once the JB Weld has dried (about 24 hours), test it to make sure the handle is secure. Then fill the remaining gaps with clay. Let dry thoroughly.

4. Test the rattle by shaking it vigorously. If the handle comes loose, you'll need to redo it. Use more JB Weld if you can, and make sure that there's a good amount between the handle and the skull; the clay is mainly cosmetic and to keep the rattling bits from slipping out around the handle.

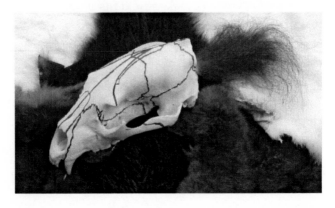

5. Once the rattle is complete, you can decorate it to your heart's content. You might try wrapping the handle in leather lacing or fur, or painting the skull with various designs.

Antler Runes

While I usually make sets of runes (elder futhark) you can adapt this for just about any set of divination symbols. Also, I recommend getting pre-sliced antlers unless you have access to a woodworking or metal shop with a band saw or similar tool; Moscow Hide and Fur (who can be found in appendix A) offers a wide variety of antler slices.

What You'll Need:

--Twenty-five antler slices of a similar size (I like them to be at least one inch in diameter)
--A Dremel with carving, sanding and polishing bits
--(Optional) Acrylic paints, small paint brush, acrylic paint sealer

1. Carve each of the twenty-four runes into one side of an antler slice. Reserve the final one either for the blank rune (which was an invention by author Ralph Blum), or as a spare.

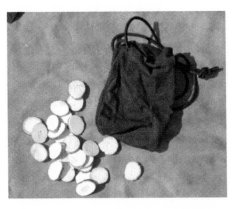

2. Sand the edges of the slices if they aren't already so that they're more rounded. Polish the runes if necessary.
3. If you like, paint the carved runes. (Or, if you're really not confident in your carving abilities, just paint them.) Seal with the spray.

Some people like to add in a little blood with the paint to be really traditional about it; however, this isn't necessary.

The drawstring pouch described in the last chapter works nicely for carrying the runes.

Bone Prayer Beads

This is mainly to introduce the concept of prayer beads using bone beads. For a truly phenomenal book on prayer beads, I highly recommend *Pagan Prayer Beads* by John Michael Greer and Claire Vaughn. It has much more detail on the mechanics, and the planning, of creating these lovely rosaries.

What You'll Need:

--Bone (and other) beads
--Jewelry wire/cord and corresponding findings/tools
--(Optional) Pendant/charm

1. Plot out the layout of your prayer beads. Will you be using these to pray to a specific being or set of beings? If the latter, should there be one bead for each, or one section of beads? Or will each bead represent an individual prayer? Perhaps you'll repeat the same simple mantra for each bead. If the bone beads are made of a specific type of bone, will you pray to the totem of that particular species? However, you plan it, make sure you have everything ready in advance so you don't run out of beads, or end up making a mistake that you don't discover until you're done.
2. If you want a pendant on a separate beaded wire than the main loop of beads, make it first. You can do this either with wire and crimp beads, or with a drop pin with an eye at the end (and make another eye at the other end once the beads are strung on the pendant wire).
3. Now it's time to string the main loop of beads. I find it easiest to start at the pendant. If the pendant will be at the center, with a

clasp opposite, I like to string both ends of the wire at the same time, alternating between putting a few beads on each side. Or, if the loop will be closed at the pendant, attach one end of the wire

 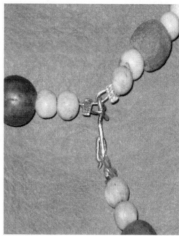

to the pendant, then string the beads around in a circle.

Left: Note the pattern of the beads, allowing for a rhythm of prayers or meditations. Right: the two ends of the wire for the lain loop are connected with the end of the pendant's wire. This is a very simple connector made with a piece of wire from a drop pin.

Deer Bone-Handled Knife With Deerskin Sheath

While you can buy premanufactured knife blades specifically for knife makers, if you already have a knife you aren't using with an easily detachable handle, this is a good option as well. Many commercial athames (especially mass-manufactured ones that aren't specifically made for a pagan market) have pommels that unscrew, and the handle and hilt then slide off. You'll want to make sure the blade has a tang (the long metal bit that is inserted into the handle).

What You'll Need:

--Knife blade

--Deer leg bone, either a tibia or femur depending on the size of the blade

--JB Weld or another industrial strength adhesive

--Air-drying clay

--Dremel with narrow sanding/grinding bit, drill bits; you may also need a long, slender chisel

--Deerskin (including lacing)

--Needles/awl and thread

--Scissors

--(Optional) Acrylic paints, paintbrushes, acrylic paint sealer

Bone-handled Knife

1. Cut one end off the bone. Prior to cutting, you may want to lay the bone over the tang of the knife to get an idea of how it will

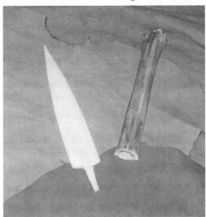

look, and how best to fit them together. If necessary, hollow out the center of the bone to make room for the tang; this can usually be accomplished with a Dremel, though if the tang is particularly long you may need to chisel out a deeper space. If you want to carve the bone with designs, now's the time to do it.

Above: Bone knife blade with carved tang, and bone handle, pre-cleaning, with end cut off and hollowed out to hold the tang.

2. Insert the tang of the blade into the bone, and make sure there's enough space for the tang to go in all the way. Then take a small piece of air-drying clay and put it in the bone. Push it down with the tang, inserting the tang all the

way — make sure the tang pushes the clay down instead of going through it! Also be sure that the clay is touching the inside of the bone on all sides; you're basically making it into a plug.

3. Mix up a decent amount of JB Weld. Insert the tang all the way in again. Then fill the bone to just below the brim with JB Weld; clean up any drips. Secure the knife in an upright position; I wrap the juncture of the handle and blade in tissue paper to keep the adhesive from leaking, then bury the entire knife blade point up in a large box of leather lacings. This is so that it is in something that is pliable enough to move around, but that will still hold the parts in place. You may find your own creative ways to keep the blade and handle secure during the drying; the most important thing is to keep them steady enough that the blade doesn't tip over and end up drying in a lopsided position.

4. Once the JB Weld is dry, fill in the rest of the gap with air-drying clay (white is preferred). You may also want to sculpt a clay hilt to cover up the juncture between the blade and handle, or wrap the juncture in leather lacing once the clay is dry. Decorate the knife however you like.

A variant I like involves hand-carved bone blades, as shown in the photos. These are much more delicate, however, and if you're just starting out I recommend metal.

Deerskin Sheath

1. Fold a large piece of deerskin in half. Lay the knife on top of the deerskin, next to the fold. Let about half of the handle extend off the edge of the skin.

2. Cut the deerskin around the knife, leaving at least a half an inch

around the edge of the knife; you'll need this slack for when you stitch the sheath together. You can leave the bottom square, or taper it to a point

3. Open up the piece of deerskin you've cut for the sheath and lay it outside-down if you'll be stitching from the outside, or outside-up if you'll be stitching from the inside. Bring the long edges together and stitch them; this will be the back of the sheath. Trim the bottom edge of the sheath to a point, then stitch shut.

4. Cut two pieces of lacing at least six inches long. Fold them over in half, and stitch or tie them to the back of the sheath, one on either side of the seam. You now have belt loops! (If your belt is more than a couple of inches wide, you'll need to make bigger belt loops.)

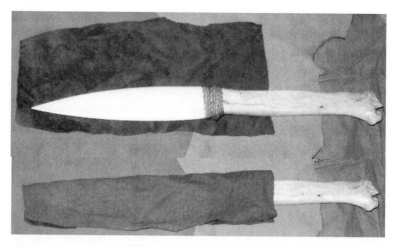

Above, top: trimming the leather to fit the knife. Bottom: Folding the leather over the knife; the edges will be stitched together down the back and the end will be tapered and stitched shut.

Right: Detail of the belt loops on either side of the back stitching.

Drilling Claws, Teeth, Antler Slices and Tips, and Small Bones

These all make nice pendants, as well as accents for other projects; additionally, antler slices make lovely buttons.

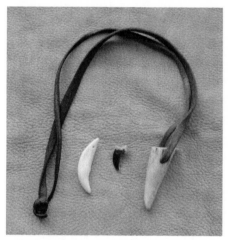

1. Put the bone to be drilled on a hard surface that you don't mind getting damaged, such as your cutting surface.
2. Select a drill bit of an appropriate size. Especially for claws and teeth don't use a larger bit than necessary; if you're just running a piece of wire through, for example, don't use the largest bit.
3. Hold the bone firmly with one hand, or with pliers, while you use the Dremel with the other. Carefully but firmly drill the hole(s) through the bone. For claws, the best spot is the center of the point where the keratin ends and bare bone begins. For teeth, drill in the thicker portion of the root.

131

Chapter Seven: Feathers

This will be a shorter chapter than the last two. In practice, feathers are not quite as versatile physically as hides or bones, but they can still make lovely accents. That and there are some neat things you can do with Borax — read on!

Feathers of a Bird

Feathers serve multiple purposes for birds. Most people will immediately think of flight when asked what feathers are for (with a few exceptions, such as the kiwi and ostrich). However, feathers also insulate and waterproof the bird's body, and additionally may act as either camouflage for protection or attention-grabbers for mating, as well as other forms of communication. Most species of bird will molt their feathers twice a year, which helps to replace damaged ones. Additionally, many juvenile birds' feathers change color with each molt as they age.

Feathers are made of keratin, the same material that horns and fingernails are composed of.[77] They evolved from scales in birds' reptilian ancestors, and in fact many newer depictions of dinosaurs show them with feathers, following the discovery of fossils of feathered dinos that also shared other physiological traits with birds. The colors of feathers may be due to colors in the keratin itself, or in nutrients the birds ingest, as well as the way light hits the feather and affects the color. Older feathers may change color as well from accumulated wear and tear.[78]

Birds generally have six types of feathers. Contour feathers include the remiges, or flight feathers on the wings, and retrices, the tail feathers. A third sort of contour feather includes the outer

---

[77] Earth-Life Web Productions, 2009
[78] University of California, 2009

layer of feathers on the rest of the bird's body. Down feathers are the soft, fluffy ones that insulate the bird, and are analogous to the undercoat of fur on some mammals. Semiplumes grow between contour feathers to aid in insulation and shape. Filoplumes look like other feathers stripped down to just a tiny tuft at the end, and these are thought to help with organizing the other feathers. Bristles are stiff, similarly stripped-down feathers that grow on the faces of some birds and protect eyes and other sensitive features. Powder feathers grow constantly instead of only molting, and are brittle at the tips, which break off regularly, creating a "powder". This powder is thought to be used in keeping the rest of the plumage clean.

When adult birds are incubating young, feathers will fall out of their breasts to create brood patches. This helps the adults to transfer heat more effectively to the young. On average there will be one brood patch for each egg laid.[79]

Where to Get Feathers

Craft supply stores almost always have at least a small selection of feathers. Common choices are pheasant body feathers (including the brown and white "almond" feathers), rooster tail feathers, various chicken body feathers, and goose feathers, both plain and dyed. Some of the suppliers in Appendix A may have a greater variety.

Because of the strict legalities involved, you may want to be very careful about picking up wild bird feathers unless you know what they are and what their legal status is. If you have access to a farm, on the other hand, it's easy to get molted feathers that are perfect for craft use. Also, if you have pet birds whose wings are clipped, you may be able to use those as well (though again, be aware of legalities).

---

[79] Earth-Life Web Productions, 2009

If you're just looking for down, cutting open an old coat or pillow may help. However, this can get very messy very quickly, not just because of the feathers, but dust made from broken down feathers, human skin cells, and even dust mites. You may want to wear a mask for this, especially if you have respiratory issues such as asthma. Outdoors is also a better location. (I found this out the hard way when I had a feather pillow explode in a dryer.)

Preserving and Caring For Feathers

The first thing you want to do whenever you get feathers from an unknown source, or that otherwise haven't been cleaned, is to debug them. Birds commonly carry mites and other pests, as well as various diseases — most of them aren't zoonotic, or transmissible between humans and other animals, but it's better to be safe than sorry.

The easiest way to kill off mites and so forth is to put the feathers into a zip-seal plastic bag and put them in a freezer for a few weeks. If you want to be extra careful, you can then clean them with a mild soap and water. While the feathers are wet, you can also fix mussed feathers, "combing" them back into shape with your fingers. Just run your fingers up the edge of the plume, from the tip of the quill (the part that attaches to the bird) to the other end. Then lay them flat to dry.

If you happen to be fortunate enough to get an entire fresh wing or tail from a bird, you can dry them with Borax. Yes, this is the same stuff that people use in laundry, though you can't use just any detergent. Make sure you have borax itself. Get a shallow box, such as the sort that department stores put clothing in, and put about an inch of borax in the bottom. Lay the wing/tail out on the borax. If you want to position it a particular way and it's being a bit stubborn, you can bury a few small pieces of Styrofoam in the borax. Then lay the wing/tail on top, and carefully use pins stuck through the feathers and into the foam to hold them in place. Once you have the feathers where you want them, put another inch of borax on top. Leave the box, covered, in a cool, dry place for at least two to three weeks; large wings and tails such as from a turkey may take longer. The borax will desiccate the flesh and keep it from rotting, as well as seal the feathers firmly into the dried flesh. (You can also use this method for bird and small animal feet, as well as mammal claws that still have skin attached.)

Do be aware that if your area has been known to have an outbreak of West Nile Virus, you're better off not messing with the carcass of a freshly dead bird. You should be handling all carcasses, bird or otherwise, with gloves, but especially in this case. If you are in a West Nile prone area in the United States, the Center for Disease Control recommends not handling the bird, and they may tell you to get rid of it.[80]

Also, while some domestic pets like to chew on hides or bones, one of my cats, Sun Ce, has an especial love for feathers. I have to keep my art/ritual room closed up, or he'll get in there and decimate the feathers that are out. Since many cat toys feature feathers, you may want to be similarly cautious with yours.

Feather Fan

Some people use these for "smudging", or directing the smoke from white sage or other burning herbs in ritual practices. They can be made with an entire dried wing or tail; however, this project just requires a few loose feathers.

You will need:

--Three to six medium to large feathers of about the same size in good condition

---

[80] Center for Disease Control, 2006

--Two pieces of flat wood at least a foot long, at least two inches wide (wider if you have larger or more feathers), and at least a quarter of an inch thick
--Glue (wood glue preferred, but white glue will work in a pinch)
--Paint, beads, other adornments (optional)
--Dremel with a saw blade or other craft saw (optional)

1. Lay one piece of wood down flat. Position the feathers at one end with the quills lying on the wood until you know about where you want them. If the feathers have especially thick quills, you may need to carve slots for them on the insides of the pieces of wood. You may also use pieces of cardboard as a template before cutting and shaping the wood itself.
2. Remove the feathers, and put a good layer of glue on the entire side of the wood that's facing up.
3. Replace the feathers where you had them.
4. Put a layer of glue on one side of the other piece of wood.
5. Carefully lay the two glued sides of wood together, being careful not to nudge the feathers as you do so.
6. Clamp the two pieces of wood together, or lay heavy books along the entire length. Let dry thoroughly.
7. If desired, decorate the wooden handle. You may also pare down the part you'll hold onto if you like; just be sure not to cut too close to the feathers. And you can wrap the handle in leather or cord for extra strength and grip.

Feather Earrings

You may not have heard of end caps; these are small bits of metal with loops on one end that are used to connect the clasp of a necklace to a cord. There are multiple types of end caps you can use for this project. One of the most common is the crimp end cap, which is pinched down, usually over a heavier cord. Another is the wire end cap, which is a small, tightly coiled wire tube in

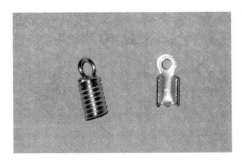

which the end of a cord may be glued. Either of these will work for this project.

You will need:

--At least one pair of small feathers
--End caps
--Earring wires
--Pliers
--Clear or electrical tape (optional)
--Glue (optional)

1. Arrange your pair(s) of feathers. You might try using more than one pair with different sizes and sorts of feather. Beyond a certain point feathers get to be too big for this sort of project, and the smaller feathers found on the bodies of birds, or smaller tail and wing feathers, are your best bet. Some larger feathers, such as peacock, may also be trimmed down for the purpose.

2. Align the tips of the quills of the feathers so they are all even. If you have a feather whose quill is long enough to make it not line up attractively with the rest of the feathers, or which would otherwise be too long, you can trim it easily with scissors.

3. Place all the quills of one set of feathers inside one of the end caps. Crimp or glue. If the combined quills are much smaller than the inside of a wire end cap, you can use a very small piece of tape wrapped around them to increase their diameter. Repeat with the other set.

4. One the glue is dry, attach the earring wires. Make sure that when the earrings hang down, the sides of the feathers that you wanted to show are facing the right way.

You can also use these as pendants for necklaces. Another variant uses aluminum "jingle cones" with the feather crimped in at one end and a loop of wire at the other to attach to the earring wire.

Feathered Mask

You will need:

--Plastic or other plain mask
--Feathers, particularly small ones from the bird's body, or flexible tail feathers such as a rooster's
--Glue
--Paint and sealer (optional)
--Glover's needle (optional)

1. If you want to paint and seal the mask, you'll want to do it before you put the feathers on.

2. Once the sealer is dry, glue feathers onto the mask. Put a dot of glue on the tip of the quill, enough to get it to stick, but not enough to be messy (You may have to experiment a bit to get it right.). Start at the top of the mask and work your way down, gluing the feathers close enough together to overlap, but not so much that they obscure each other. Glue them in the direction feathers would grow if people had them, with the tips of the quills facing down toward the jawline. Try and contour the direction of the feathers with the contours of the face. If you're really

138

ambitious, you can use a glover's needle to carefully poke holes in the mask to put the quills through, but this is incredibly time-consuming. However, they'll be more securely fastened (assuming you still glue them).

Painted Feathers

Painting a feather can be as simple as altering a white goose feather to look like a hawk or eagle feather, or as elaborate as painting an entire scene.

You will need:

--A large wing or tail feather, such as from a white goose
--Paint and sealer

1. Using small amounts of paint, thinned with water if necessary, carefully paint on the top side of the feather. You may find it easier to paint with the "grain" of the feather; be careful not to muss the grain.
2. Let the paint dry. Then spray with a succession of very light, quick coats of acrylic sealer, letting each one dry thoroughly before applying the next.

Chapter Eight: Skindancing

While I talked about other ritual practices involving skin spirits earlier in the book, I wanted to give a chapter specifically to skindancing, as it's one of the most elaborate and complex forms of magic related to them. Skindancing is a form of shapeshifting that combines invocation with sympathetic magic. It involves wearing the skin of another animal in order to shapeshift to that particular species. It's obviously impossible to physically shift, apart from a few modern anecdotes among therianthropes[81] and others of minor changes in eye color and facial structure that consistently coincide with mental/spiritual shifts. However, the skindancer's perception may change so dramatically that s/he may be convinced that s/he actually has taken on the form of the animal in all ways. Additionally, a good skindancer can be convincing enough in taking on the movements of the animal that s/he may convince onlookers that the animal walks among them in the flesh.

This last point may seem impossible, and in our regular state of consciousness it is. However, magic requires altered states of consciousness, and in group situations this includes the spectators as well as the participants. While on one level everyone understands that before them is one of their friends or neighbors in costume, pretending to be the animal, on another it is understood that the animal has manifested through the ritual.

---

[81] For those who've never heard this term, a therianthrope is a person who believes that in some manner (generally nonphysical) s/he is a nonhuman animal. S/he may have been that animal in a past life, or may feel that some part of hir psychology more resembles the animal than human. For more information, both *Fang and Fur, Blood and Bone* and *A Field Guide to Otherkin* have chapters on therianthropy. You may also surf over to http://www.werelist.com. The next chapter also deals with therianthropy in relation to totemism.

Joseph Campbell sums it up: "[T]here has been a shift of view from the logic of the normal secular sphere, where things are understood to be distinct from one another, to a theatrical or play sphere, where they are accepted for what they are *experienced* as being" (italics his).[82]

Mircea Eliade agrees: "For primitive man, donning the skin of an animal was becoming that animal, feeling himself transformed into an animal...Little would be gained by recording the fact that shamans dressed up in animal skins. The important thing is what they felt when they masqueraded as animals".[83] Historically animal skins have been a part of ritual regalia (shamanic and otherwise) in cultures around the world. While we have only speculation to back up the details, it is thought that the animal-human hybrids found in the cave of Les Trois Freres in France may have been shamanic figures representing those who created magic for a successful hunt.[84] The physical shamans themselves may have inspired the paintings through wearing skins of animals previously hunted as a way of helping repeat the success.

In more modern times, animal skins and other parts are used in the ritual regalia of a number of Native American tribes. These are formal outfits rather than daily wear (the famous eagle feather war bonnet was not something that was worn 24-7!) and today they are primarily reserved for powwows and tribal ceremonies. For example, the men's northern traditional style of dance performed at pow-wows may call for regalia that includes an animal skin headdress.[85] And one ceremony that the Tsimshian tribe may use upon the creation of a new totem pole features a dance by a person dressed in a goat's skin and handmade mask.[86]

---

[82] Campbell, 1984, p. 21-22.
[83] Eliade, 459.
[84] Campbell, 1998, p. 73-79.
[85] Littlecrow Trading Post LLC, unknown date
[86] Vitebsky, 79

However, some Native artists have continued to create traditional everyday clothing, and this as well as the more formal regalia often incorporates furs and other parts.

In most cases, shapeshifting was not the primary purpose of the ceremonial garb of various global societies, though the incorporation of animal parts may have been a way of honoring a group totem or animal spirit, depending on the culture and the individual. The shamans and other magic workers of many cultures, however, incorporated animal symbolism into their clothing and other magical items, often as a way of connecting with that animal. While these were often masks and other pieces of costumery not directly derived from the animal hirself, there are cases where partial or whole skins were used in sympathetic magic.

While not universal, animal skins have been found in shapeshifter lore around the world. For example, several European rituals for becoming a lycanthrope involve wearing a partial or full wolfskin. Skinwalkers, the malign entities of several southwest Native American tribes, also sometimes utilized coyote or other skins. And the Norse "Berserker" translates literally as "bear-shirt" for the bearskin that was worn (the wolf "Berserker" was actually known as an Úlfhéðnar.[87]

Skindancing and Multi-Layered Totemism

Skindancing is an intense act of magic, and when combined with totemism can be incredibly potent. It allows you the chance to really feel what it is to be that animal, at least as much as is possible while incarnated in a human body.

Animal totems, in my experience, are archetypal beings that embody all of the qualities of a given species. This includes not only the natural history, but also the mythology and lore and

---

[87] Lupa, 2007

other human attention given to the physical animals—as well as the relationships between humans and the totem's species. They are not just individual animal spirits, but watch over those spirits, whether incarnate or not.

Wearing an animal skin is a form of sympathetic magic, as mentioned above. It makes a very strong connection in the mind of the dancer—and anyone watching the ritual—between the magic that is happening, and the animal being worked with. The prevalence of the energy of that animal aids the process of evoking or invoking the corresponding totem. The skindancer may find that the totem easily slips into hir body, guided by the costumery, while onlookers may choose to encourage the totem's arrival through evocation rites. Even if the skin isn't worn, it can be a receptacle for the totem to reside in for the duration of the evocation, or it can act as a permanent home in a sacred place.

However, the totem isn't the only animal entity to keep in mind when dealing with skins and other remains. As discussed previously, the animal parts have spirits of their own. It's quite possible to work with the spirit of the skin and the totem together. As I've mentioned, I see three general explanations of what a totem is: an archetypal being, an individual animal spirit, and a psychological aspect of the self. While I tend towards the archetypal/psychological theories, for the purposes of the following concept I'm going to also include the skin spirit under "totemism".

Let me give you an example. A while back, I wanted to work some magic to bolster my job hunting efforts. I'd been feeling rather discouraged, and even a bit self-sabotaging, and wanted to reverse that trend. You can apply for all the jobs in the world, and get as many interviews as you can, but if you go in with a negative attitude you may as well have stayed home. So it was time to counteract the self-sabotage I'd indulged in.

I went to my skins and I asked, "Who can help me with this?" The badger spoke up: "I can teach you how to make your efforts more efficient, and find a means of living that you'll gain a lot from". He showed me an image of a hole in the ground with a neverending supply of grubs, mice and other things that badgers find delicious, the closest he had to show as a parallel between what I wanted and what a badger thinks of as a good supply of resources. Not that I expect to end up with a hole full of grubs, of course.

That's where Badger the archetype came in. Once I opened the ritual and evoked all my friends, family and guardians, I called on Badger and told him of my need. He understood perfectly and was able to communicate further to my badger skin spirit what exactly the objective was.

As I was performing the ritual, I also called upon that within me which is badger in nature. Pretty much every time invoke an animal energy I astrally shift to that animal for as long as the invocation lasts. As I went through the various processes of my magic, I could feel (nonphysically) the silver and black fur over my skin, the way that a badger's limbs are shorter, and the muscle more compact, with a sharp-toothed muzzle. However, the more abstract connections also came to the fore; I felt more grounded and strong, less afraid of the task at hand.

This wasn't the first time I'd used the tri-layered approach; for years I've done totem dancing with a wolf skin, calling on the archetypal Wolf, the spirit of the skin, and my own lupine nature as I danced. It was the first time I'd ever worked with Badger, though. In the past, when working with a new totem, I just called on the archetype; for example, in previous job hunting rituals I had called upon Otter and Beaver, but only through evoking the archetypal totems. The connection to Badger in this ritual was a lot stronger, though time will tell what the full results of the ritual will be.

It would be easy for me to simply say that these were separate beings, that the Badger archetype was entirely independent of the badger skin spirit, both of which were unconnected to the internal badger aspect. And some would argue that one was a totem, another a spirit guide, and the third just a figment of my imagination. However, I see them as all connected, as I see all of reality connected. That which we label as Badger manifests in numerous ways, on one level Badger is the archetype; on another, Badger is every physical specimen of several species of mustelids; and on a third, Badger is that within me (and possibly other people) that not only relates to the furry animal that can dig a burrow quicker than a person can shovel, but also the ideas of tenacity and resourcefulness. This increases the power of the totem and also allows a more personal connection because of the physical contact with the skin, and the invocation of the badger-self.

Which Animal to Start With?

You have three basic choices. You can start based on the totem, you can start based on the skin spirit, or you can get feedback from both. It's entirely up to you. I've been dancing Wolf (and my current wolfskin) since 2002 mainly because that's my primary totem and therefore an animal that I have a lot of connection to. However, I've danced plenty of others over the years, and I intend to keep experimenting with different dances.

It's a good idea to start with a totem you're comfortable with, because it reduces the amount of adjusting you have to do — otherwise not only do you have to get used to allowing another entity to interact with you through invocation, and the shifts in perception and mindset that often follow, but you also have to get to know this new animal that you may have had no prior contact with. There aren't any animals that are necessarily easier or harder to work with, though some people may find it easier to identify with BINABM like wolves, deer, bears and the like.

A lot depends, too, on what your purpose is. If you want to deepen the relationship with a totem or become more like a certain animal on a long term or permanent basis, then the choice is pretty obvious. However, if you're dancing for a specific need, you'll want to find a totem who specializes in what you're working with. You might come up with a couple of different options and then talk to each of them.

This is most easily done for a lot of people through guided meditation. I have found that the standard one used for finding your totem that just about every book that talks about totemism can be altered to contact pretty much any animal spirit or entity. It's primarily a matter of intent; if you go down into that tunnel seeking, for instance, Koala, you're probably not going to run into Zebra (unless they've both decided that Zebra would be a better choice).

You may also feel unusually drawn to a particular totem that has chosen you. It's usually pretty obvious when this sort of thing happens — totems are good at dropping subconscious hints that leak into our everyday consciousness. Still, if you do feel compelled to work with a specific totem, double-check your feelings first. You can be pretty good at fooling yourself, especially if there's an animal that you really, really want to work with, but which may not be appropriate for the time and place you're at.

Skin spirits can be pretty communicative, too. There have been plenty of times where I've been walking through a shop that sells skins and other remains and felt a very strong "ping" on my intuition, only to trace it to a particular skin that really wanted to go home with me. I've ended up working with both skin spirits and their respective totems that I never would have guessed I'd connect with because of this. So if you get a particular skin that decides s/he absolutely must go home with you, it's a good idea to listen. (If the price is a bit above what you have, see if the person selling the skin has a lay-away program.)

You may find that it's best to consult both the skin spirit and the corresponding totem to get both of their perspectives.

Regardless of who you choose to dance with first, make sure you're comfortable with your choice. If you find you've been chosen, and you aren't entirely comfortable, then communicate that to the spirit and/or totem who's chosen you. You may need to get to know them better before proceeding.

Dancing With a Skin, Or...?

Skindancing, as I've developed it, generally is done with a whole pelt. I've already discussed how to make a dancing skin. However, skindancing can be done with even the smallest bit of fur or bone; a single tooth on a cord can be effective.

Part of the fun and pageantry of skindancing, though, is the costumery aspect of it. (Imagine that—ritual being fun!) A whole hide is a lot more dramatic than a single tooth, and if for no other reason than sheer psychology can have a greater effect on the dancer and other participants because of that. On the other hand, a lot of small bits and pieces can be combined to make a big, impressive dance costume. Scraps of fur can be stitched together with pieces of bone, feathers and other remains to make a composite costume honoring many skin spirits and totems.

Also, as mentioned, you don't have to use actual animal remains to get the same effect in skindancing. Just so long as the artificial replacements are properly prepared, you can have every bit as effective a costume as someone with a whole hide.

The Art of Skindancing

Now comes the really fun part—learning to dance with the skin, its spirit, and the totem. I suggest working with the skin spirit first, since s/he'll be present at all times regardless. If you're working with a real skin I suggest doing a purification ritual before attempting any other communication as a form of respect. While it's rather stereotypical, I do like purifying animal parts with sage smudges; we all like the smell, and it does do a good job of clearing the energy. However, use whatever method you prefer. Just be aware that water-based methods may damage the fur or other parts, especially if soaked for too long. Sprinkle a little water rather than immersing the skin in it.

Next, spend some time just talking with the skin spirit. Put aside a little time each day to meditate with hir, and see if s/he's ready to dance yet. It's important that you're both ready and comfortable with the idea; nobody likes being forced into anything, magic included. If you're nervous yourself, you may find that talking to the skin spirit can help calm you down and make the idea of dancing seem more appealing. Similarly, spend time working with the corresponding totem, getting to know hir.

Once you're both ready, get your dancing area ready. If you want drumming or other music, turn it on. You may also want to dance in the nude if you're in an appropriate setting; I prefer it as it gives me a better connection with the skin. Make whatever other preparations you might like, such as getting some water to have on hand. Then put the skin on. I like to make it a bit of a ritual. With my whole wolf skin, for instance, I first put my arms through the foreleg holes in the skin. I then bind the hind paws to my ankles, and imagine that the lower half of my body has turned into that of a wolf. I bind the forelegs and forepaws to my arms and hands, and visualize my torso and arms becoming lupine. Finally, I pull the head and neck up over like a hood, and the transformation is complete.

Now it's time to dance. Start to move like the animal as best as you can. My arms are way too short for me to comfortably move around in a quadruped manner but I can hunch down with my back relatively parallel to the ground and move my arms like forelegs. If I'm at a drum circle I let the drums carry me into the rhythm, allowing my movements to match those of the drumbeats. If you choose to skindance at a drum circle, just be careful of other dancers, especially once you get deeper into the shift.

Of course, you don't have to make your first foray into skindancing in front of a bunch of people. In fact, the safety of your own home is a good idea for a couple of reasons. First, it gives you privacy, which helps the self-conscious and also offers a lack of interruption (especially if no one else is home). It's also a familiar place; lots of external changes can distract you from your magical experimentation. It can take time to learn how to move gracefully with a hide strapped to your limbs. And it's a good place to be if something does go wrong.

Wrong? What could possibly go wrong? Mostly the same things that can go wrong with any form of invocation. Allowing any entity, even an animal spirit, into yourself can be a powerful experience, especially if you're not used to it. I've never had any trouble with totems or other animal spirits taking me into full trance possession; they've always been very respectful of my boundaries. That doesn't mean that everyone else's experiences will be the same. If you do feel that things are getting overwhelming, stop dancing. Turn off whatever music, if any, you're dancing to, remove the skin, and leave the room. Eat something protein-heavy to ground you, and just sit for a minute or two to come back to this reality. Then go back in and check on the skin spirit, and wait a few days before you try again.

While most pagans are sane, responsible people, I have met a few throughout the years who have struck me as particularly in need of attention. They want all eyes on them, and they'll make the most outlandish claims to get what they want. Unfortunately, this isn't always a conscious act on their parts. In the case of shapeshifting magic in general, I've seen people who have claimed that their totem (almost always a predatory BINABM) possessed them against their will all of a sudden and made them run around scaring children or trying to bite people. When asked why they didn't stop it, they whine "But I caaaaaaan't!" In the cases where I've seen this happen, it was quite clear that it was the person hirself doing stupid things while blaming the totem.

149

It's one thing to experience trance possession during a Voodoo ritual or similar ceremony, in which possession is encouraged and expected. However, there are certain hallmarks of true possession, and the officiators of the ritual can tell pretty quickly who's faking it. As for random possession by entities in general, that's more the stuff of Hollywood demons than reality. In the rare case where you do have a particularly persistent and pernicious pest trying to get your attention through possession or other influences, you should be learning how to shield yourself and communicate on your own terms before you even think of working with shapeshifting.

I can't really describe what it feels like to be fully shifted, and everyone's experience is different, so I can't really give you a fair warning of what to expect. For me, there is a moment when I feel the skin spirit merge fully with me, and we share body and skin alike. Once that occurs, nothing else in the entire Multiverse matters. There's a definite sense of euphoria accompanied by an adrenaline rush, but the rest is beyond words.

Once you're familiar with shifting with the skin spirit and can do it pretty consistently, you can also invite the totem to join you, either through evocation or invocation. I do this at one of two points in the skindance. I may evoke the totem before the dance begins and ask hir to dance alongside me for the duration of the ritual, or sometimes at the peak of the shift I invite hir to join me and the skin spirit in our dancing through invocation. The latter can be an incredibly powerful experience due to the sheer concentration of energies that are combined together. It takes practice to be able to invoke multiple entities at once, and I suggest working with skin spirits and totems of the same species to avoid too much conflict.

When the dance is done, and you've banished and said farewell to the totem and allowed the skin spirit to return entirely to the skin, make sure you ground yourself. Follow the instructions I gave a few paragraphs ago about stopping the dance. Then record your results, and give yourself some time to process what happened before trying again.

So I've Shifted — Now What?

Most of the material about totemic shifting talks about the process of getting there, but not so much what to do once you've hit the desired state of consciousness and magic. While shifting in and of itself is an amazing experience, once you're used to being in that state there's plenty of magical potential.

For example, say you've lost an object or need to find a piece of information, and you're having trouble locating it. You might consider working with African Wild Dog, Lion, Wolf, or another group-based predator, skindancing to become that animal, and evoking a pack or pride to work with you and increase the "eyes" looking for what you seek. In fact, if you're feeling really ambitious you could create a group of servitors in the form of a particular group-based species, with you as the dominant animal, for routine work.[88]

Shielding or warding your home while shifted allows you to bring forth the territorial instincts that almost every species of animal possesses. Predators aren't the only animals that defend their territory, either, though they may be more aggressive about it if the prey population is low. Depending on how elaborate your skin is, and how tolerant your neighbors are, you can either go around the perimeters of the outside of your house (or the building your apartment is in) or simply make a circuit of the interior. Pay especial attention to places where intruders may enter more easily, such as doors and windows. Feel free to mark your territory as you see fit; while you may not want to urinate on the carpet, you can leave a few strands of hair at various intervals. You can also use energy to mark the boundaries of your home;

---

[88] I go into more detail about this in *Fang and Fur, Blood and Bone*.

over time just the residual energy of you walking past the same places over and over can help build up the boundaries.

If you're just planning on evoking a totem into your ritual area, rather than invoking hir into your self, shifting can help facilitate the process. I find that when I'm shifted to a particular species that I communicate with the corresponding totem differently. The thoughts flow more easily without the encumbrance of so many words, and it's a lot more instinctual.

Sometimes skindancing can simply be an offering to the totem, especially if invocation is included. If your skin is relatively unobtrusive, or you have access to some private land where nobody will care if you're "outlandishly dressed", you might invoke the totem and the skin spirit and take them both for a run through the wild areas. I also enjoy doing this at drum circles at pagan gatherings. It's pure celebration anyway, and allowing the animals to join in just makes it better as far as I'm concerned. This sort of skinshift is a joyous revel, feelings the animal within, the animal in the skin, and the totem animal all united amidst the rhythms of the drummers and dancers.

Skindancing can also be incorporated into other more elaborate systems of magic. As a part of shamanism, for example, skindancing can cause the altered states of consciousness used in journeying. It can also be a vehicle for one's helping spirits to channel their aid. And, again, skindancing as offering can be useful here.

Once you're more adept at skindancing, you'll find that it's a lot easier to do on short notice. For example, I've been working with Wolf for so long on so many levels that shifting more towards a lupine mindset literally happens in an instant. Eventually you'll find that you'll be able to shift without the aid of the skin at all (though this leaves the skin spirit out of the fun). You'll also discover that you can shift to varying degrees, from a very light hint of the totem, all the way to a full invocation. Being able to shift on short notice and to a specific point can be useful.

152

The almost clichéd example is a person walking down a lonely street at night, feeling threatened, and shifting to a predatory animal to scare away a potential mugger. However, if you're a healer and you have an injury or illness to tend to, you might lightly shift to whatever totem you work with in your healing work. Or if you're feeling nervous before a job interview, call on a totem that speaks of bravery to you, or prosperity.

Obviously if you have a full skin you can't take it with you everywhere you go. You might consider creating a second, smaller portable skin out of a small scrap of fur or fabric, or blessed jewelry. I have a wolf tail that fits nicely into my carryon bag, and enjoys the chance to get out and go places with me. Just be sure to treat it in the same manner as your full skin, and understand that it has its own independent spirit within.

Conclusion

This book is the result of over a decade of artistic, spiritual, and magical work. Perhaps more than any other part of my practice, it is a system that I have personally developed because there were no guidelines available to me. While I always have and ever will encourage innovation on the part of my readers, I hope that this text gives you a good starting point for working with animal parts. Just as an artist starts out with foundational texts and then over time develops hir own personal style, my intent is for you to get the basic toolkit for the work described within so you can then take it and add your own customization, both on artistic and spiritual/magical levels.

If you have any questions, I do try to be accessible as an author. My primary website (where, among other things, my artwork may be viewed) is http://www.thegreenwolf.com. I also spend a lot of time on Livejournal as lupabitch. And my email address is whishthound@gmail.com. Additionally, while I'm a busy person, I do try and make it out to pagan festivals and other events, mostly in the Pacific Northwest, but occasionally elsewhere (especially if festival coordinators are willing to help me get out there!). If you happen to run into me in person, I love talking shop (which is one of the main reasons I wrote books in the first place, to be honest).

Afterword

But Lupa, you already wrote a conclusion!

Well, yes. But it was suggested to me by my foreword writer, that this (originally a Livejournal post) would make a good afterword to this text. And, having thought about it, I thought he had a great idea. So here it is.

I did some repair on my wolf dancing skin while I was near the end of completing this book, the skin on page 113.And I've come to the conclusion that I'm going to have to retire him pretty soon. On the fur side he looks intact. However, he's falling apart. I had to patch a number of tears on the skin side, and the hide was too weak to stitch--I had to glue leather over the tears. He's been deteriorating for a few years now, but now he's falling apart at some crucial places; I repaired a long rip at the armhole. This is probably the last repair job I can do on him and still have him functional for dancing.

I've had him for around a decade or so. I didn't take the best care of him that I could have the first few years I had him, even after we started dancing. Too many rainy festivals, plus the heat from fires at drum circles, took their toll, and he doesn't care much for the damper weather here. I knew he'd wear out sooner than a skin kept in a more climate-controlled setting, but it's still sad that the time has come.

He was the first wolf hide I ever got; I actually paid for him on layaway because I was a student at the time. He's also the very first hide I ever danced with. It just worked so perfectly; he's a big enough skin, and I'm a small enough person, that my arms fit through the holes at the forelegs like a coat, and I could tie his back legs to my ankles and still have his head draped over mine. We fit together so nicely, and it made dancing him incredible. Every time we danced, I felt his spirit meld with mine, and we became one being, human and wolf together.

And people really appreciated it. I forget how many compliments we've gotten, people saying how they felt Wolf there at the circle, how inspired they were. I remember one little girl at a pagan festival site who was enthralled every time she saw us dance; normally I don't let other people touch the wolf skin, but I let her drape him over her head, and she got her picture taken by her dad--and it just made her day.

I thought it was silly of me, for a moment, to be getting so upset over a worn-out dead wolf hide. And yet I had people—including people who don't even subscribe to a pagan spirituality—supporting me in this, allowing me a place for that grief. It's not just the grief for a *thing*, but for a being, a spirit. And it's mourning the loss of being able to dance the first skin I ever danced, which went a long way in helping me develop the material in this book and in my practice at large.

The skins and bones—they have meaning to me. And maybe that's what this is all really about, acknowledging that meaning as a part of a spiritual and/or magical path. Our beliefs center on what is important to us, and these remains are important to me. My wolf skin has a lot of value, not for what he originally cost, but for the many years we've spent together, the many times around the fires with the drums pounding and our paws on the dirt.

"Retirement", for this old wolf hide, won't mean being thrown out. It'll mean getting a special place to rest, probably on a permanent Wolf altar I want to create. I'll most likely do a final dance ceremony for him. And then it'll be time to introduce the new wolfskin, and start making a relationship with that one. And I'm already looking for a replacement, though it'll be a while before I can save up enough--a full large wolf hide with the feet and claws intact, big enough for me to wear all the way to my ankles, costs a few hundred dollars, and it's harder to justify that expense for a skin I won't be selling.

But for right now, I'm going to cherish the last few dances I have with my old wolf, and plan a good retirement ceremony for him.

Appendix A: Where to Get Skins, Bones and Other Animal Remains

This list is comprised of companies that sell animal remains of various sorts, generally brand new. For secondhand, try local thrift stores or antique shops. eBay and other online auction sites may also yield good finds, though be aware that bidding can be fierce! Additionally, if you happen to have a Livejournal account, join the community at http://furhideandbone.livejournal.com, whose members frequently buy, sell and trade animal parts.

Moscow Hide and Fur
PO Box 8918
Moscow, Idaho 83843
Phone: 208-882-0601/fax: 208-882-5715
CustomerService@hideandfur.com
http://www.hideandfur.com

These folks are my main choice; they're wholesalers so their prices are good, and they've always been quite willing to include all the necessary paperwork, such as CITES forms. They have a spectacular selection as well, and you can order individual skins, bones and other parts on their website. Highly recommended, and incredibly helpful. I tend to favor them for CITES species, since they're good about supplying paperwork on request, even for incomplete hides and so forth.

Eidnes Furs
83363 Hwy 3 So.
St. Maries, ID 83861-7175
(208) 245-4753/fax (208) 245-5358/(888) 233-4366 (orders only)
furman@usamedia.tv

http://www.eidnesfurs.com

Some of Eidnes Furs' prices are spectacular, though they're reasonable in general. You can also get discounts for buying in bulk. Their selection isn't quite as good as Moscow Hide and Fur, but for some things you can get a much better deal. The biggest down side is that you can't select the exact things you want to buy, though if you're looking for something specific, try asking them for help—very good customer service.

FurTail
alambada@yahoo.com
http://www.furtail.com

This online-only wholesaler specializes in more common tails, paws and faces at the absolute best prices I've seen online. Quick shipping, really good quality stock for the prices, and an all-around good resource.

Black Bear Haversack
2204 Elm
Granite City, IL 62040
Contact form on website
http://www.black-bear-haversack.com

Decent selection and prices, with some items you won't find anywhere else. Good shopping cart system; you can order however many of something that you want, though you won't get to pick individual things. Good customer service, too.

Sioux Trading Post
P. O. Box 8303
Rapid City, South Dakota 57701
800-541-2388
Contact form on website

http://www.siouxtrading.com

Some of the nicest people in the world are at this shop. It's the best place I've found to get John James glover's needles, my favorite type for stitching leather and fur. Their selection of furs and such isn't that large, but they do tend to carry top quality. They have lots of other nifty things as well, so it's worth poking around their site (or shop, if you're there in person).

Tandy Leather Factory
U.S. Phone: 1-800-433-3201
International Phone: 1-817-496-4874
Canada Phone: 1-800-450-3062
http://www.tandyleatherfactory.com

This is the big daddy (or mama, if you prefer) of leather and leather working supplies. While they don't have a lot besides leather, they specialize in tools for working various sorts of leather, especially the heavier-grade tooling leather; lots of neat tools and toys here. Their prices are sometimes kind of steep, and shipping is downright exorbitant. However, the up side is that they have dealers all across the U.S. as well as Canada and the United Kingdom, so if you have one in your area it's worth it to go to in person and save the shipping. Many of the dealers don't have the Tandy Leather brand in their name, just for the record.

The Bone Room
1569 Solano Ave.
Berkeley, CA 94707
(510)526-5252
evolve@boneroom.com
http://www.boneroom.com

While their prices aren't as good as Moscow Hide and Fur, they specialize in the weird and exotic. They have everything from replicas of fossils to really hard to find skulls and bones from around the world, and they're infamous for selling legal human bones. Go here to get things you can't find anywhere else.

Cedar Mountain Drums
2237 East Burnside St.
Portland, OR 97214
(877) 34 DRUMS
Contact form on website
http://www.cedarmountaindrums.com

This is a wonderful drum shop in Portland, OR. Not only do they offer a wide variety of pre-made drums made with elk, deer, moose, horse and bison hides, but you can choose from a nice selection of kits, as well as drum making components. The owner is quite knowledgeable about drums and drum making, so shoot any questions you may have his way. If you end up being a flop at making drums, you can always pick up a drum already made and ready to play. (My personal shamanic drum came from this place!)

Appendix B: Animal-Based Nonprofits

Yep, I'm still being lazy. This is basically the same list from *DIY Totemism*, which I lifted from *Fang and Fur, Blood and Bone*, with a few minor changes. Expect this list (changed as necessary) to continue showing up in all my books on animal magic in some incarnation or another.

The Defenders of Wildlife
National Headquarters
1130 17th Street, NW
Washington, DC 20036
USA
1-800-385-9712
defenders@mail.defenders.org
http://www.defenders.org

The Defenders of Wildlife work to protect wild species, large predators in particular, worldwide. Programs include not only population growth but also habitat preservation and endangerment prevention. I donate a portion of the money I make on my artwork to these folks.

American Society for the Prevention of Cruelty to Animals (ASPCA)
424 E. 92nd Street
New York, NY 10128-6804
USA
(212) 876-7700
http://www.aspca.org

Royal Society for the Prevention of Cruelty to Animals (RSPCA)
Wilberforce Way
Southwater
Horsham
West Sussex
RH13 9RS
United Kingdom
0300 1234 555/+44 870 33 35 999 (international calls)
http://www.rspca.org.uk

Scottish Society for the Prevention of Cruelty to Animals
Kingseat Road
Halbeath
Dunfermline
KY11 8RY
United Kingdom
03000 999 999
http://www.scottishspca.org

Royal Society for the Prevention of Cruelty to Animals Australia
PO Box 265
Deakin West ACT 2600
Australia
02 6282 8300 (or 61 2 6282 8300 outside of Australia)
http://www.rspca.org.au

The SPCAs in general are aimed primarily towards the welfare of domestic animals, though the various branches do sometimes have campaigns involving wildlife. They do a lot of work towards educating the public about issues and proper domestic animal care. Also, I added in the information for the Scottish SPCA as I had a reader inform me that they are independent of the Royal SPCA and apparently receive very little funding from that group (and so can always use the donations!)

Humane Society of the United States (HSUS)
2100 L Street, NW
Washington, DC 20037
USA
(202) 452-1100
http://www.hsus.org/

While the Humane Society is best known for pet adoptions, the organization has extensive campaigns for domestic and wild animals alike. If you're in the United States and you're looking for a pet, check out your local Humane Society shelter.

World Wildlife Federation (WWF) International
Avenue du Mont Blanc 1196
Gland
Switzerland
+41 22 364 9111
http://www.panda.org

One of the best-known wildlife preservation organizations, the World Wildlife Federation has spent the past four decades working with issues on a global scale. They focus a lot on both species and habitat based programs, and include the needs of indigenous cultures in their solutions for worldwide problems.

The Wilderness Society
1615 M St., NW
Washington, D.C 20036
USA
1-800-THE-WILD
http://www.wilderness.org

This organization specializes in protecting wildlife habitats; keep in mind that many of the animals facing extinction today are endangered because of habitat loss.

Natural Resources Defense Council
40 West 20th Street
New York, NY 10011
USA
(212) 727-2700
http://www.nrdc.org

Another good organization that lobbies for habitat and species protection, as well as helping more local groups protect areas near them.

Animal Welfare Institute
PO Box 3650
Washington, DC 20027
USA
(703) 836-4300
http://www.animalwelfare.com

A more moderate group than some, this organization nonetheless has been seeking better treatment of animals in the wild, in labs, and in agriculture since 1951.

The Jane Goodall Institute

4245 North Fairfax Drive
Suite 600
Arlington, VA 22203
USA
(703) 682-9220
http://www.janegoodall.org

Founded in 1977 by one of the foremost authorities in biological field research and the behavior of chimpanzees in the wild, the Jane Goodall Institute works to not only protect chimps and their habitats, but to educate people worldwide about animal welfare, conservation, and what we as individuals and communities can do to help animals, both wild and domestic. The JGI features a variety of innovative programs of interest.

Bibliography

Books

Brown, Joseph Epes (1997). *Animals of the soul: Sacred animals of the oglala sioux*. Rockport, MA: Element Books.

Campbell, Joseph (1984). *The masks of god: Primitive mythology*. New York: Penguin Books.

-- (1988). *Historical atlas of world mythology, volume one: The way of the animal powers, part one: Primitive hunters and gatherers*. New York; Harper & Row.

Davies, Lucy and Mo Fini (1994). *Arts and crafts of south america*. London: Thames and Hudson.

Davis, Wade (1985). *The serpent and the rainbow*. New York: Warner Books.

Ellwood, Taylor (2006). *Inner alchemy: Energy work and the magic of the body*. Stafford, U.K.: Immanion Press/Megalithica Books.

Feest, Christian F. (1994). *Native arts of north america*. New York: Thames and Hudson, Inc.

Galenorn, Yasmine (2004). *Totem magic: Dance of the shape-shifter*. Berkeley: The Crossing Press.

Greer, John Michael and Claire Vaughn (2007). *Pagan prayer beads: Magic and meditation with pagan rosaries*. San Francisco: Red Wheel/Weiser.

Hart, Mickey, with Jay Stevens (1990). *Drumming at the edge of magic: A journey into the spirit of percussion*. San Francisco: HarperSanFrancisco.

Hawthorn, Audrey (1994). *Kwakiutl art*. Seattle: University of Washington Press.

Jones, Evan John and Clifton, Chas (1997). *Sacred mask, sacred dance*. St. Paul: Llewellyn Publications.

Landeen, Dan and Jeremy Crow (1997). *I am of this land (Wetes pe m'e wes): Wildlife of the hanford site (a nez perce nature guide)*. Washington: Nez Perce Tribe Environmental Reconstruction and Waste Management Department.

Lupa (2006). *Fang and fur, blood and bone: A primal guide to animal magic*. Stafford, U.K.: Immanion Press/Megalithica Books.

-- (2007). *A field guide to otherkin*. Stafford, U.K.: Immanion Press/Megalithica Books.

-- (2008). *DIY totemism: Your personal guide to animal totems*. Stafford, U.K.: Immanion Press/Megalithica Books.

O'Neill, Claire (1994). *The oracle of the bones*. New York: St. Martin's Press.

Searfoss, Glenn (1995). *Skulls and bones: A guide to the skeletal structures and behavior of north american mammals*. Mechanicsburg, PA: Stackpole Books.

Stebbins, Robert Cyril and Cohen, Nathan W. (1997). *A natural history of amphibians*. Princeton, NJ: Princeton University Press.

Taylor, Colin (1998). *Buckskin & buffalo: The artistry of the plains indians*. London: Salamander Books.

Telesco, Patricia and Hall, Rowan (2002). *Animal spirit: Spells, sorcery and symbolism from the wild*. Franklin Lakes, NJ: New Page Books.

Triplett, Todd (2003). *Small game taxidermy: How to work with squirrels, varmints and predators*. Guilford, CT: The Lyons Press.

Whitcomb, Bill (2008). *The magician's reflection*. Stafford: Immanion Press/Megalithica Books.

Websites

Anonymous (2009-A). *Animal trapping*. Retrieved 16 August, 2009 from http://en.wikipedia.org/wiki/Animal_trapping.

Anonymous (2009-). *Bone*. Retrieved 16 August, 2009 from http://en.wikipedia.org/wiki/Bone/

Anonymous (2009-). *Skin.* Retrieved 16 August, 2009 from http://en.wikipedia.org/wiki/Skin.

Center for Disease Control (2006). *West nile virus: What you need to know.* Retrieved 16 August, 2009 from http://www.cdc.gov/ncidod/dvbid/westnile/wnv_factsh eet.htm.

CITES Secretariat (2001). *How CITES works.* Retrieved 18 July, 2008 from http://www.cites.org/eng/disc/how.shtml.

--. *What is cites?* Retrieved 18 July, 2008 from http://www.cites.org/eng/disc/what.shtml.

Defenders of Wildlife (2008). *Wolves lose protection under endangered species act.* Retrieved 18 July, 2008 from http://www.defenders.org/newsroom/press_releases_fold er/2008/02_21_2008_wolves_lose_protection_under_endan gered_species_act.php.

Department of Vertebrate Zoology, National Museum of Natural History (2001). *Encyclopedia smithsonian: The passenger pigeon.* Retrieved 18 July, 2008 from http://www.si.edu/ Encyclopedia_SI/nmnh/passpig.htm.

Draper, Electa (2009). *Eagle bodies, parts for indian rites are collected, sent from colo. morgue.* Retrieved 4 September, 2009 from http://www.denverpost.com/ci_13242945.

Earth-Life Web Productions (2009). *The wonder of bird feathers.* Retrieved 16 August, 2009 from http://www.earthlife.net/birds/feathers.html.

Eggers, Audrey (2002). *Farming for fur.* Retrieved 16 August, 2009 from http://www.furcommission.com/farming/foxfarming.htm.

Engber, Daniel (2006). *Where do zoo animals go when they die?* Retrieved 17 August, 2008 from http://www.slate.com/id/ 2134941/.

Fish and Wildlife Services (2008). History and evolution of the endangered species act, including its relationship to cites. Retrieved 18 July, 2008 from http://www.fws.gov/endangered/ ESA/esasum.html.

-- (2002). *A guide to the laws and treaties of the united states for protecting migratory birds.* Retrieved 18 July, 2008 from http://www.fws.gov/migratorybirds/intrnltr/treatlaw.ht ml.

-- (unknown). *Bald eagle protection act of 1940.* Retrieved 18 July, 2008 from http://www.fws.gov/laws/lawsdigest/ baldegl.html.

-- (unknown). *Marine mammal protection act of 1972.* Retrieved 18 July, 2008 from http://ipl.unm.edu/cwl/fedbook/ mmpa.html.

Friends of Animals (2008). *Fur farms.* Retrieved 16 August, 2009 from http://friendsofanimals.org/programs/fur/fur-farms.html.

Ghosh, Nermal (2002). *The tiger bone market.* Retrieved 16 August, 2009 from http://www.forevertigers.com/tigerbone.htm.

Heath, Chris "Count von" (1996). *Brainballs, skulls and warrior (The celtic cult of the head.)* Retrieved 18 August, 2008 from http://www.whitedragon.org.uk/articles/headcult.htm. Originally published in White Dragon magazine, Imbolc 1996.

Humane Society of the United States (1998). *Questions and answers about fur.* Retrieved 16 August, 2009 from http://files.hsus.org/webfiles/PDF/WILD_Questions_and _Answers_about_Fur.pdf.

Littlecrow Trading Post, LLC (unknown). Pow-wow dance styles. Retrieved 16 August, 2009 from http://www.littlecrow tradingpost.com/pagestyle.htm.

Montgomery, Delia (2001). *Fur ethics.* Retrieved 16 August, 2009 from http://www.furcommission.com/resource/perspect99as.htm.

National Oceanic and Atmospheric Administration Office of Protected Resources (unknown). *Marine Mammal Protection Act (MMPA) of 1972.* Retrieved 18 July, 2008 from http://www.nmfs.noaa.gov/pr/laws/mmpa/.

United States Congress (1973, etc.). *Endangered species act of 1973.*

Retrieved 18 July, 2008 from http://epw.senate.gov/esa73.pdf.

--(1940, 1999). *Bald (and Golden) Eagle Protection Act (of 1940).* Retrieved 18 July, 2008 from http://permits.fws.gov/mbpermits/regulations/BGEPA.PDF.

-- (2001). *Title 50 – Wildlife and fisheries.* Retrieved 16 August, 2009 from http://frwebgate.access.gpo.gov/cgi-bin/get-cfr.cgi?TITLE=50&PART=20&SECTION=91&YEAR=2001&TYPE=TEXT.

University of California (2009). *Are birds really dinosaurs?* Retrieved 16 August, 2009 from http://www.ucmp.berkeley.edu/diapsids/avians.html.

Various (2005). *Furhideandbone: Hey, what's the best way to clean a bird skull?* Retrieved 16 August, 2009 from http://community.livejournal.com/furhideandbone/88876.html.

Various (2009). *Furhideandbone: Smelly, greasy skulls.* Retrieved 16 August, 2009 from http://community.livejournal.com/furhideandbone/467988.html.

About the Author

Lupa lives in Portland, OR with her[89] husband and fellow author, Taylor Ellwood, their cats Sun Ce and Ember, and more books and art supplies than any human being should probably share space with. She has been known to leave her abode to grace the presence of her long-term other significant other, S., as well as to carry on a torrid sadomasochistic love affair with graduate school, by which means she hopes to obtain a Master's degree in counseling psychology.

In addition to being an author, she is also an editor, layout tech, and promotions/publicity manager for Immanion Press/ Megalithica Books, the upstart small press who didn't mind her yammering on about animal sacrifice and people who think they're really dragons. She is a semi-professional book reviewer at http://www.paganbookreviews.com, as well as for Witches & Pagans magazine and Thorn magazine. Lupa also is an artist (in case you skipped the rest of the book just to read the bio) and makes ritual tools, jewelry, and other sacred art out of animal bones, feathers, hides, and other remains.

As though she doesn't have enough to do already, Lupa is also developing a non-core neoshamanic path based on her experiences and research, and aimed at addressing the needs of the culture she is a part of. Details may be found at http://therioshamanism.com

The truly Lupa-addicted may find her at http://www.thegreenwolf.com.

---

[89] Yes, she's using female pronouns this time around.

Did You Like What You Read?

Women's Voices in Magic by Brandy Williams (editor)
ISBN 9781905713394/MB0139
$20.99/£11.99 paperback
Shattering the stereotypes of women as only supporting figures in ceremonial, chaos, and other male-dominated magical communities, this anthology features essays from a wide variety of female practitioners.

Liber 767 vel Boeingus by Jozef Karika
ISBN 978-1-90571-34-0/MB0140
$21.99/£12.99 paperback
Slovakian chaos magician Jozef Karika distills over fifteen years of intense experimentation in this text of entity work and germs, sigils and pop culture, and a good dose of laughter (and not only for banishing!).

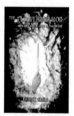

The Flowering Rod by Kenny Klein
ISBN 978-1-905713-28-8/ MB0128
$21.99/£12.99 paperback
Is Paganism a women's religion? What is the role of men in Paganism and Wicca? Priest, summoner, student, teacher, how can men fulfill these roles and worship the Pagan God by themselves, in groups of men, and in groups of men, women and children?

Talking Abut the Elephant edited by Lupa
ISBN 978-1-905713-24-0/ MB0125
$21.99/£12.99 paperback
Cultural appropriation is an increasingly hot topic in neopaganism. This collection of essays explores a wide range of positions on how we borrow from other cultures, and the effects this can have.

Find these and the rest of our current lineup at http://www.immanion-press.com

Lightning Source UK Ltd.
Milton Keynes UK

176566UK00002B/4/P